T0349352

Advance Praise for
The Future Boardroom

"The world needs innovation. The status quo is not working and needs urgent attention, as many symptoms of systemic failure are appearing. Corporate boards will play a strategic role in addressing these issues, displaying both humility and courage. Helle Bank Jorgensen's book will help individuals and boards to do this and demonstrate that business as a force for good is not just a statement but a positive affirmation of a successful future for humanity."

André Hoffmann, Vice-chair of Roche Holding, and board trustee of the World Economic Forum

"Board members need to make earning trust a priority in their counsel to CEOs struggling with geopolitics and societal issues. Stakeholders are looking to business as the most competent and most ethical institution. *The Future Boardroom* is an invaluable playbook for directors."

Richard Edelman, CEO of Edelman

"Amid turbulence and uncertainty, Helle Bank Jorgensen's book offers valuable insights to future-proof the boardroom, drawing on interviews with seasoned governance experts. A must-read for any (aspiring) board member aiming to stay relevant and amplify their impact."

Katell Le Goulven, Founding Executive Director, Hoffmann Institute, INSEAD

"With her deep insights into the role and responsibilities of corporate boards, *The Future Boardroom* is a must-read for board directors who want to serve companies and their communities to their full potential. It is an easy-to-read book that captures the complexities and perceived dilemmas of today's business world with deep insight and clarity, and with plenty of real-life examples it is an important tool for current and future NEDs wanting to make a difference on the boards they serve. Do not miss out on this book!"

Pia Heidenmark Cook, Non-executive director and senior advisor (former CSO at Ingka Group/IKEA)

"With growing expectations on boards, *The Future Boardroom* offers a clear and comprehensive guide to effective governance for the years to come. Helle Bank Jorgensen elevates performance over mere compliance, tackling key issues like sustainability, board dynamics, and leadership. Covering everything from stakeholder engagement to the vital role of the chair, this book is an essential resource for boards and their advisors."

Lloyd Mander, Chair – Membership Committee, Institute of Directors in New Zealand

"We have entered dark times of disruption, instability, and unthinkables. This means acute new pressures on board directors that most don't feel able to contemplate, let alone equipped to handle. This is why they must read at speed *The Future Boardroom*. Helle's advice is brutally frank but also encouraging. If you are not prepared to think and prepare for the unthinkable in radical ways, then you must ask: Am I suited to being a director? This book will go a long way to ensuring you are a valuable and responsible one."

Nik Gowing, Founder and director, Thinking the Unthinkable

"This book is a masterclass in forward-thinking leadership and innovative governance. Helle Bank Jorgensen channels decades of experience into a visionary guide that not only addresses today's complex global challenges but also inspires board members and corporate leaders to embrace transformation. Her insights bridge the gap between traditional boardroom practices and the urgent need for sustainability, technological savvy and inclusive decision-making."

Sibylle Barden, Author; host of Der Große Neustart
(The Great Reset) podcast platform

"*The Future Boardroom* is an essential guide for boards navigating today's turbulent business environment, offering a compelling roadmap for integrating sustainability into the core of corporate governance. With real-world examples and expert insights, Bank Jorgensen masterfully outlines how boards can transform to meet emerging challenges by embedding sustainability into every aspect of decision-making. She emphasizes that sustainability is not just a compliance issue but a fundamental driver of long-term value creation. In a world where resilience and responsibility are paramount, *The Future Boardroom* is a clarion call for boards to embrace sustainability as a strategic imperative."

Jingdong Hua, Vice-chair, International Sustainability Standards Board

"*The Future Boardroom* is an impressive and insightful handbook for business leaders, and is much needed at a time of continuing confusion, and sometimes consternation, over the role of business in society. Helle has brought fresh thinking on the role of individual directors and the board as a whole. She also gives clear direction for leaders on delivering financial performance backed by strong governance and sustainable practices in an increasingly volatile world. And she's done this without shying away from the tricky political, technological, and social questions that every leader needs answers to in this age. This book is a must-read for 2025."

Lindsey Stewart, Director of stewardship research and policy, Morningstar Sustainalytics

"This timely book presents a compelling vision of boardroom evolution. The author masterfully draws parallels between corporate governance and political representation, offering a fresh perspective on directors' responsibilities to their stakeholders. The metaphor of Mother Nature's invoices brilliantly illustrates the urgency of climate action at the board level. Through practical guidance and thought-provoking questions, the book equips directors with the tools to navigate the transition between present and future challenges."

Maali Khader, Chief executive, Middle East
Institute of Directors

"The quest to become a great director is a never-ending journey—and a serious part of our ongoing growth and development. Helle's book is a terrific resource to support us on that journey."

Kathleen Taylor, Chair, Element Fleet Management;
former chair, Royal Bank of Canada; former president
and CEO, Four Seasons Hotels and Resorts

"As a board these days, you have to accept that business is not only about markets but also about politics, culture, and so many other facets of our lives. Helle recognizes how the job of a board is changing, and her book identifies the opportunities which arise as this transformation unfolds."

Torben Möger Pedersen, Chair, Copenhagen Business School

"Helle Bank Jorgensen has created a must-read book for board members and all those concerned with the workings of boards now and into the volatile years that lie ahead. This is a beautifully clear, elegantly concise and thoroughly authentic book—a sheer pleasure to read. I loved the real-world examples shared by Competent Boards alumni and faculty and the deep insights provided by renowned experts across the globe."

Michael Jenkins, Author of *Toxic Humans: Combatting
Poisonous Leadership in Boards and Organizations*

"Helle is one of the most sensitive and erudite professionals I know. This wonderful book focuses on making boards future-ready by adopting the qualities of diligence, thoughtful participation, respect for fellow board members, an equal voice for every member, and a willingness to expend time and energy on the boards one serves on. Her chapter on the chair's leadership is particularly important."

Shailesh Haribhakti, Independent director, Lafarge Holcim group

"We cannot solve tomorrow's problems with yesterday's board. Anyone who thinks their board is fine is most likely already losing. As we demand more from our CEOs, so should we from our boards. This book will be a useful check on whether you pass the test or can do better. I suspect it's the latter. As the role and importance of business increases in line with the global challenges we need to address, so does the need to have a high-performing, engaged, and connected board. This book will help you get there."

Paul Polman, Former CEO, Unilever; former chair, International Chamber of Commerce

"Helle draws on the advice of experts with real life experience in doing not the easy governance things but the things that are hard. Her book is an easy read with a compelling narrative. It can be a very useful reference for all directors and for the boardroom table. I commend her for writing this valuable book."

Phillip Meyer, Chair, Australian Financial Services Group

"The pace of change is accelerating, and board members today face complex and intersecting challenges of climate change, sustainability and technological change. These are not only rapidly transforming our world but often raise crucial ethical and reputational issues that can impact companies profoundly. *The Future Boardroom* will clarify, assist, and guide board members in dealing with these challenges."

Jane Diplock, Supervisory board member, Global Reporting Initiative and World Benchmarking Alliance; director, Singapore Exchange Regulation; deputy president, Abu Dhabi Appeals Board

"In a world of fragility, fear, and fractured landscapes, Helle highlights the need for curiosity, courage, and collective responsibility. She encourages us to embrace the future with confidence, viewing board service as a purposeful opportunity to learn, contribute, and champion values that shape a brighter future. Helle inspires us to leave our organizations better than we found them. Unlock your true potential and transform the future of boardrooms with this inspiring read."

Katherine Garrett-Cox, Chief executive,
GIB Asset Management; chair, Clean Air Fund

"In *The Future Boardroom*, Helle Bank Jorgensen captures the essence of what it means to lead in today's rapidly changing world. This book is a compelling call to action for boards to embrace change, technology, lifelong learning, to harness the wisdom of next-generation talent … and much more."

Faisal Kazi, CEO and president, Siemens Canada

"*The Future Boardroom* is a masterful guide to navigating the complexities of modern corporate governance. Helle Bank Jorgensen's insights are both profound and practical, offering a roadmap for leaders who aspire to drive sustainable success in turbulent times. This book is an essential read for any board member committed to excellence and innovation."

Maureen Metcalf, Founder and CEO,
Innovative Leadership Institute

"The challenges facing corporations today are increasingly complex and, in many cases, unprecedented. Helle has created a practical playbook for board members, guiding them to ask the right questions—not only of management teams but of themselves as well. This is an essential resource for any board looking to optimize its effectiveness. Bravo!"

Eric Wetlaufer, Board Member TMX Group,
IMCO, Enterra Solutions

HELLE BANK JORGENSEN

THE

HOW TO TRANSFORM IN TURBULENT TIMES

FUTURE
BOARDROOM

BARLOW BOOKS
fine books for enterprising authors

Also by Helle Bank Jorgensen
Stewards of the Future: A Guide for Competent Boards

Library and Archives Canada Cataloguing in Publication data available upon request.

ISBN: 978-1-998841-23-3

Printed in Canada

Publisher: Sarah Scott
Book producer: Tracy Bordian/At Large Editorial Services
Copy editor: Dawn Loewen
Cover design: Paul Hodgson
Interior design and layout: Ruth Dwight
Indexer: Audrey Dorsch

For more information, visit **www.barlowbooks.com**

Barlow Book Publishing Inc.
96 Elm Avenue, Toronto, ON
M4W 1P2 Canada

My mother, Ellen, passed away in Denmark on September 4, 2024,
as I was working on this book.
I will be forever grateful for all she taught me and all she did for me.
She was a steward of the past, of the present, and of my life.
She lives on in my heart,
and this book is dedicated to her memory.

CONTENTS

Why This Book Matters—Turbulent Times Ahead   xv

1 A New Era in the Boardroom   1

2   Wanted: A Fresh Approach   27

3 The Shifting Governance Landscape   55

4 Road Map to the Future   73

5 Competence, Curiosity, Courage, Compassion...   95

6 Who Should Be at the Future Boardroom Table?   121

7 Technology: Master or Servant?   137

8 From Shareholders to Stakeholders   165

9 The Wise Chair   185

10 A Plan of Action   199

Thank You   213

Endnotes   217

Index   227

About the Author   235

WHY THIS BOOK MATTERS— TURBULENT TIMES AHEAD

Business leaders have rarely, if ever, faced as turbulent a landscape as they do today. Disruption and uncertainty are coming at them from every direction—politics, technology, economic volatility, Mother Nature, and their stakeholders of today and tomorrow—all making the task of a corporate board more complicated, but also much more important.

No fewer than seventy-three national elections were held in 2024, and many resulted in a sharp change in political direction. Most notably, we saw Donald Trump win a second term as US president on a platform that promises upheaval on a scale seldom seen in a modern democracy. In other parts of the world, from Britain and France to Mexico, Iran, and South Africa, voters have sent an unmistakable signal that they are fed up, not only with their political leaders but with their entire system of government.

Far from the world we had envisaged of tumbling trade barriers, concerted action to combat climate change, and improved living standards for all, we have been battered by an enormously costly pandemic, destructive wars and natural disasters, festering inequality, and, as 2025 unfolds, a new wave of trade protectionism. With the rise of political polarization and economic isolationism, corporate leaders are shying away from their earlier embrace of progressive social policies, encapsulated in the two abbreviations ESG (environmental, social, and governance issues) and DEI (diversity, equity, and inclusion).

It's hardly surprising that I'm asked with mounting frequency whether these shifting sands mean that the drive for corporate sustainability that I have long championed has stalled or, even worse, crashed and burned.

My answer is an emphatic *No*. On the contrary, as the world transforms, businesses and their boards must equip themselves with the insight, foresight, and networks to navigate the new risks and opportunities that they face. Business leaders need to be able to communicate what is best for their company in the short and long term. They need to learn to look around corners and to communicate the future consequences of past and present missteps.

This book aims to encourage the adaptability and resilience that boards will need to see them through these turbulent times. So buckle up. As a board director and as a leader, you have a choice whether to leave your company and the society it depends on in a better or worse state than you found them.

I will argue it is our role as stewards of the company and stewards of the future to leave the company and the society in a better state than when we joined the board—and I hope this book will help guide board directors and leaders around the world to do exactly that. Leave the society the company depends on in a better state. Or else, well, the company will not be in a better state.

Unfortunately, too many boards are far from ready to confront the once-in-a-century disruptions that are upending our lives and our businesses. Many board members tell me that they do not really understand how younger generations think. They acknowledge that they have yet to digest the full implications of the wave of populism that has swept across the globe in recent years, not to mention the power of social media and the explosion of mis- and disinformation and fake news. Most of us have failed to realize that the logic of a boardroom discussion does not necessarily apply to people struggling to put food on the table who have lost hope in a brighter future. To make matters worse, our planet has started to send some costly invoices in the form of devastating floods, droughts, hurricanes, wildfires, and loss of biodiversity.

Many of the challenges that boards now face were barely on the horizon when I founded Competent Boards in 2018. It's a tribute to the far-sightedness of business that, as of January 2025, more than 1,250 directors and senior executives in over 57 countries are part of the Competent Boards network, helping them not only to transform their own careers but to bring lasting benefits to their companies and their communities. I have been honoured to share my insights on podcasts and expert panels, and to deliver keynote speeches at numerous high-profile events around the world. It has been a privilege and pleasure to guide boards towards making the world a better place for themselves and our children to live in.

Nevertheless, the task remains a daunting one. A Competent Boards survey in late 2024 revealed that only 16 percent of corporate directors were "very prepared" for the potential regulatory and governance changes likely to flow from the recent spate of elections, especially in the US and Europe. This is a dangerous state of affairs not only for the companies that boards serve, but for society as a whole.

In this book I have tried to answer such thorny questions as: What changes can we expect in society that will alter the way boards work? What will be the purpose of the board of the future? Who should be around the boardroom table? What will the skills matrix of the future boardroom look like? What will shareholders, employees, suppliers, customers, and indeed society at large expect of boards? How should they do their work and use their influence within the company and in society at large? How can they be masters rather than servants of exciting but also risky new technologies? How will we structure the business of the board in future? In what ways can the board work better? In summary, how can the boardroom of today transform into a better boardroom for tomorrow?

Importantly, the chapters that follow also offer some pointers for directors willing to do more than just collect a cheque. My message is that those who choose to merely *sit* on a board have no business being there. If they are doing their jobs properly, they must *serve* on the board. By doing so, they will make their businesses fit for both resilience and sustainable growth while making the world a much better place for all of us. To every director with the courage to serve in the future boardroom, I say: the experience will be well worth your time and effort, but, be warned, it will not be a walk in the park.

To appreciate the scale of the challenge, imagine a corporate board of twelve members as a microcosm of our planet. Six of the directors would be men and six women, and three-quarters would be under the age of fifty. Two would be people with disabilities (bearing in mind that 16 percent of the world's population has a disability). At least one would have a mental health or substance abuse disorder (representing an estimated 13 percent of the world's population). Two would be from India, two from China, two from Africa and one from Europe and one from Americas. Two or three directors would be living beneath the poverty line, and one would call home a place that is likely to be submerged by rising oceans and frequent floods. Finally, eleven of the twelve board members would live in highly polluted parts of the planet (based on 99 percent of humans living in places with unhealthy levels of air pollution).[1] And the younger those directors are, the more likely they are to be worried about being exposed to even more pollution, even more catastrophic floods, hurricanes, and wildfires, and even more devastation to the bounty of nature.

I guarantee that no corporate board on earth can boast such an equitable composition, and few should. But those facts and figures serve a useful purpose in that they illustrate the vast challenges facing the future boardroom. They have also guided me in taking a fresh look at the duties and responsibilities of corporate directors with the aim of identifying who are part of the problem and who are likely to emerge as part of the solution.

The Economist did not mince its words in summing up the dire prospects facing the world in a May 2024 editorial:

> For years the order that has governed the global economy since the second world war has been eroded. Today it is close to collapse. A worrying number of triggers could set off a descent into anarchy, where might is right and war is once again the resort of great powers. Even if it never comes to conflict, the effect on the economy of a breakdown in norms could be fast and brutal.[2]

Such a sobering prognosis should set alarm bells ringing in every boardroom. It presents every corporate director with a stark choice: Do I simply let the future unfold and risk ending up in a worse spot than we already are? Or do my board colleagues and I seize the initiative and try to navigate our company and our community through the looming storm? Most directors will surely choose the latter course. After all, that is what their stakeholders expect of them, and what they are paid to do.

My previous book, *Stewards of the Future*, first published in January 2022, sought to describe the fast-moving world in which corporate directors find themselves. It outlined the challenges posed by climate change, human rights, artificial intelligence, biodiversity, and the 17 sustainable development goals agreed to by 193 member states of the United Nations. It warned boards of their growing responsibility for their companies' supply chains, and the urgent need for more diverse thinking in the boardroom and senior management ranks. My goal was to help directors and other business leaders understand the tremendous risks and opportunities facing them. I've been grateful to hear that it has changed mindsets and has guided many boardroom decisions, spurring innovation and transition plans, reimagining products and business models, and improving the reputations of companies and those that lead them.

This book is different. In addition to hinting at *what* the future may look like, it focuses on *how* directors, both individually and collectively, can and must transform their boardrooms to ensure that they swim rather than sink in the treacherous waters now swirling around them.

///

Those waters are approaching from multiple directions. Our planet is sending urgent signals that it has a finite capacity to provide the resources that we have up to now taken for granted. Banks and other lenders are reassessing their exposure to assets in danger of being stranded by climate change. Property insurers are warning about the heightened risk of floods and wildfires, and pulling the carpet from under homeowners who can't afford rising premiums or cannot sell the houses that were once seen as their retirement funds and have now become golden prisons or, in business terms, stranded assets. Providers of directors and officers liability insurance are looking at how they price the heightened risk of lawsuits. Malevolent players in cyberspace are forcing companies to constantly be on guard against sophisticated cyberattacks. Artificial intelligence and quantum technologies are demonstrating both the rewards and the risks of innovation.

In addition, businesses and their directors are under scrutiny as never before, whether from government regulators, shareholders, social and environmental activists, employees, customers, and even their own children and grandchildren. Corporate managers find themselves in the awkward situation these days of children asking if it is true what their playmates say at school about their parent working for a business that destroys nature and the child's future quality of life.

All of us—especially young people—have every reason to be frightened and angry about the future, and corporate boards would be foolish to ignore those fears. Some far-sighted business leaders are under no illusion about the trouble we're in. One of the first to do something about it was the late Ray Anderson, founder of Atlanta-based Interface, one of the world's largest makers of carpet tiles and a heavy petrochemicals user. Anderson had an epiphany in 1994 as he was researching a presentation on the environment for his sales staff. He realized, as he later recalled, that "I was running a company that was plundering the earth. I thought, 'Damn, someday people like me will be put in jail!'" Anderson vowed that Interface would shrink its carbon footprint and other environmental costs to zero by 2020. He died in 2011, but his Mission Zero lived on, so much so that Interface met the target a year ahead of schedule. It has remained a leader in sustainability. For example, it now uses a waste product from discarded car windows as a component in its carpet tiles. In partnership with the Zoological Society of London, it buys discarded fishing nets from poor communities, using them to create new yarn.[3]

I've also been struck by the story of Ørsted, the Danish renewable energy company. Formerly known as Danish Oil and Natural Gas (DONG), Ørsted has transformed itself from a fossil-fuel-based energy company into a global leader in renewable energy. Over the course of a decade, it divested its fossil fuel assets and invested heavily in wind and solar energy. By 2020, it had slashed its carbon emissions by 83 percent compared to 2006 levels and aims to reach a 99 percent reduction in 2025.[4] Ørsted's wind farms currently supply clean energy to millions of homes around the world, and *Corporate Knights* magazine has recognized it as the world's most sustainable energy company.[5]

Regulators around the world are gradually stepping up the pressure for change. A tsunami of new disclosure requirements, standards, and restrictions have swept across the corporate world in recent years. Close to half the directors and executives who answered the Competent Boards survey about the impact of the 2024 elections take the view that boards will face even tougher reporting and oversight requirements in future.

Then there are the legal challenges. A growing number of countries now recognize Mother Nature as a legal person and ecocide as a crime. As a result, more and more board members have found themselves in the crosshairs of lawsuits accusing them of not doing enough to protect the environment, even as others are accused of putting nature before short-term shareholder returns.

I gave a talk a few years ago to a group of students enrolled in a sustainability management program at the University of Toronto. As a way of illustrating how business has responded to the climate crisis, I proudly told them about the time I worked with Maersk, the big Danish shipping company, and how we managed to shrink its carbon footprint by instructing vessels to reduce speed. I had barely finished my story when one of the students put up his hand. I was expecting to hear a gracious compliment for our pioneering work, but instead he ever-so-politely laid into me for my and Maersk's lack of imagination. Hadn't we fallen into the trap of "old thinking"? he asked. After all, the vessels were still being powered by diesel fuel—and large quantities of it too. Hadn't we considered equipping the ships with wind turbines or some other kind of renewable power? Why hadn't we shown more imagination?

Brief though that interaction was, it made a lasting impression on me. That young man may not have had the most practical answers to Maersk's problems. (In fact, the Danish company has turned out to be a leader in expanding the market for "green" fuels that produce very low greenhouse gas emissions.) But he clearly understood that the best way to find solutions to seemingly intractable challenges is by fearlessly questioning traditional assumptions and pushing towards new horizons, no matter how distant or unfamiliar. That is precisely the message I have sought to impress upon corporate directors since setting up Competent Boards in 2018, and it is another key theme of this book.

III

The need to step up the pace of change in the boardroom has never been more urgent. Business now finds itself on the front line of issues that will define humanity's future, and every enterprise, no matter how big or small, has a role and responsibility to help move society in a sustainable direction.

Furthermore, it is no longer sufficient to identify a problem and look for ways to remedy it. Every company should be examining its entire business model, asking to what extent it is contributing to society's problems and how it can make a positive contribution towards addressing them. To their credit, many companies are discussing transition plans to reach net-zero greenhouse gas emissions by 2040, 2030, or sooner. But far fewer are considering the larger question of how to reinvent their business and the products they make to ensure a sustainable future.

I had the privilege of working with Danish Steel Works in the 1990s to produce the world's first green account integrated into an annual financial report. One of the questions I asked my boss at the time was why the steel (which was produced by recycling old material) was sold and not leased to the buyer. I was told that leasing would be too cumbersome and that the regulations and accounting standards made it all but impossible. Plus it was not possible to separate the materials afterwards. All that was true back then, but the government later mandated producers to take back electronics after use and recycle the materials, a requirement that made research, development, and product design far more rewarding. In today's world, with its emphasis on reuse, recycling and circularity, a lease model may make more sense than throwing away materials. This applies to cellphones, clothes, and, yes, even steel. All it needs is a different mindset.

Whether for good or ill (perhaps a bit of each), there's no denying that the business community has the potential to be one of the most powerful forces for change in global politics, commerce, and culture. Of the world's one hundred largest financial entities, almost seventy are corporations. As of late 2024, only five of the world's roughly two hundred countries—the United States, China, Japan, Germany, and India—had economies (measured by gross domestic product, GDP) larger than Apple. Walmart's market value sat between the GDPs of Canada and Spain. The products and services of companies like Alphabet, Amazon, Meta, Microsoft, Samsung, SpaceX, and Tencent (owner of WeChat) have become an essential part of our daily lives. These and hundreds of other multinationals have the financial clout, the global reach, the engagement with consumers and suppliers, and the lobbying and communication skills to make an impact far beyond their own factories and warehouses. Even much smaller businesses can be influential agents for change in their own communities if they are willing to harness the resources of their various stakeholders—employees and their families, suppliers, customers, distributors, and, not least, financial backers.

Unfortunately, the fractious nature of public discourse these days and the rise of extremism, on both the left and the right of the political spectrum, have made it difficult for lawmakers to push through a sensible, middle-of-the-road agenda, especially if it involves any pain for voters, no matter how short-lived. Whether it's immigration policy in the US, human trafficking in Southeast Asia, or human rights in China, governments have been either unable or unwilling to tackle many of their citizens' most pressing concerns. The so-called "elites" have become so comfortable in their secluded communities, their fancy cars, and, yes, their boardroom chairs that they have failed to notice what is happening in the world around them. Their lofty ideals and carefully reasoned arguments have done little to reassure ordinary folks trying to make their voices heard. As the rise of populist movements shows, we are now all impacted.

Yet enlightened and determined corporate boards can prod their companies, whether public or family-controlled, into making a tangible contribution towards a brighter future for society. Like a sports team that switches players during a game, a board can change directors and maintain account-ability without jeopardizing the company's stability or its sense of purpose. And just as a smart coach gives a winning team coherence and continuity, a wise chair can keep a board and, by extension, a company pointed in the right direction. The wise chair will keep abreast of the latest trends in soci-ety and know what people on the street need and are talking about. Some down-to-earth street smarts and common sense would not go amiss. If more businesses move forward in this way, society as a whole will benefit from their talents, their resources, and their ideas.

The power of business to make the world a better place is amplified by the fact that it can often move the needle in ways that governments can't. Whether separately or together, companies can act more boldly and more quickly to create a sustainably level playing field. One of my goals in writing this book is to give boards the courage and the tools to stand up for their principles.

A commitment to stakeholder governance puts a heavy responsibility on corporate boards. As the late Ratan Tata, one of India's most prominent and thoughtful business lead-ers, put it: "Business needs to go beyond the interest of their companies to the communities they serve."[6] But expanding a board's horizons in this way demands new and often unfamiliar skills. Directors need to keep asking themselves not only what they want their company to achieve but what kind of world they want their company and its stakeholders to live in. The director of the future must have the courage to ask tough questions on such complex issues as energy transition and security, corruption, artificial intelligence, quantum technology, societal, including demographic changes, cybersecurity, and human rights in the supply chain.

Unfortunately, that degree of curiosity and insight is still lacking around many boardroom tables. All too often, the assumption remains that the CEO can be left to put a strategy in place to transform a corporation in a way that meets today's needs. While it is true that the CEO runs the company, the ultimate responsibility for transformation will always lie with the board. It is the directors' job to set the parameters for change, to hire a CEO who will get the job done, and then to keep assembling information and asking questions to ensure that the agreed-upon strategy is carried out. I regularly find myself calling out directors who tell me that they "sit" on the board of company ABC. No, I tell them. You do not sit. You serve.

I hope that this book will provide the insights you need to make your board more resilient and adaptable for turbulent times, a board that is truly fit for the future.

CHAPTER ONE

A New Era in the Boardroom

I don't expect businesspeople to be saints. But they also have to be very cognizant of where the limits are. They should always ask themselves, at the very least: How would you feel if this becomes a front-page investigation by the FT or some other newspaper?

—*Martin Wolf*, Financial Times *chief economics commentator*

The winds of change are blowing through the corporate world with a ferocity that I never imagined when I sat down in early 2021 to start work on *Stewards of the Future*, my book on the role of a corporate director in the twenty-first century. Extreme weather patterns, rising shareholder activism, political polarization, threats to water supplies and other natural resources, the risk of the next pandemic, cyberterrorism, quantum technology, geopolitical tensions ... these are just some of the pressures that are forcing companies around the world to rethink their business models, redesign their products and supply chains, engage more actively with local communities, and re-examine their governance models, culture, incentives, and internal controls. To add to the challenges, we are undoubtedly still closer to the beginning than the end of this disruptive process.

At the centre of the maelstrom is the board of directors. With the tenure of the typical chief executive now measured in years rather than decades, it falls more than ever to the board to guide the company through these turbulent times. "Monitoring the progress of transformations, learning from mistakes and learning from different outcomes along the way to make sure that the same pitfalls aren't recurring have become essential parts of every board's work," says Kathleen Taylor, former chief executive of Four Seasons Hotels and Resorts and former chair of Royal Bank of Canada. At the same time, Taylor adds, every transformation is accompanied by risk, "and so boards need to be attuned to figuring out how much risk is associated with any proposed transformation and set themselves up to properly oversee the process."

In later chapters we will explore these new realities and how boards can adapt to them without causing more harm than good. For now, it is worth delving into the forces that have brought us to where we are.

SHIFTING PRIORITIES

We often hear board members insist that their fiduciary duty is solely to shareholders. However, their responsibilities and the perception of those responsibilities have expanded dramatically over the past decade or two, and are sure to expand even further in years to come as the realization sinks in of the wide impact that a corporation has and the benefits that it draws from society as a whole. Thus, it comes as no surprise that more than three-quarters of the 444 directors who responded to a 2024 survey by BCG, the INSEAD Corporate Governance Centre, and Heidrick & Struggles believe that boards have a responsibility to address broader societal concerns.[7] Although 54 percent of the survey's respondents still believe that business objectives should remain their primary focus, almost a quarter said that boards should give as much, or even more, priority to societal concerns. Or, as Phillip Meyer, chair of Australian Financial Services Group, puts it: "Harry Hindsight is not serving on my boards." Indeed, the people I would most want on a board are Freddie Foresight and Ingrid Insight.

To take just one example of what is expected from today's corporate directors, the Canadian Bar Association has noted that modern slavery laws are opening new avenues of liability, requiring directors to approve and sign disclosures related to forced labour and child labour.[8] Even if directors are not directly liable, current reporting requirements have heightened the risk of their being held liable for breaches of their fiduciary duty. Directors are now exposed to allegations that they have failed to act with reasonable care, skill, and diligence when signing an anti-slavery statement, or failed to exercise due diligence in determining what steps their company should take to address the risk of modern slavery in its supply chain.[9]

The board of the future will have to move away from traditional "reactive" responsibilities to a much more proactive view of what its role should be. Instead of merely keeping the business afloat, directors will be under an obligation to leave the company in a better place than where they found it. In doing so, they will have to decide what "success" looks like and how it should be measured. Ensuring sustainability will form an increasingly important part of that work. As the Brundtland Commission put it in 1987, sustainability means "meeting the needs of the present without compromising the ability of future generations to meet their own needs."[10]

Of course, compliance with laws and regulations will still be part of the future board's agenda, but only as a "check-the-boxes" item rather than a constant focus of attention. Instead, board meetings will quickly move on from compliance matters to a more productive discussion of strategy and how to solve short-term challenges in a manner consistent with the company's long-term purpose, vision, and plans. Foresight, imagination, and an eagerness to be a positive force for good will be key.

Boards will be looking further and deeper into the future than they do today, helped by technology that their forebears could only dream of. I foresee the day when directors will meet in the metaverse world of shared and immersive virtual networks much as teenagers connect now on their virtual reality headsets. They will examine different scenarios that their colleagues have prepared based on input from management and their own research. To an ever-greater extent, board members will be encouraged to ask "What if?" questions, and then test the answers against the many variables that may influence the business. They will debate their values and beliefs, and then decide how willing they are to steer their company into virgin territory.

NEW THREATS BRING NEW CHALLENGES

The list of unfamiliar issues facing today's board members is a long one. In what seems like the blink of an eye, artificial intelligence has moved from the realm of science fiction to a mainstream technology with a universally understood abbreviation: AI. Inflation, after being confined to economic history books for more than three decades, returned with a vengeance during the COVID-19 pandemic and remains a worry. Interest rates soared, credit tightened, and workers became more aggressive in their demands for higher wages. Energy security has been propelled onto board agendas by a variety of developments, including European countries' efforts to wean themselves off Russian gas, the decommissioning of fossil fuel power plants, the economics of renewable energy sources, and the huge amount of electric power required by AI data centres. Import tariffs and other forms of protectionism are increasingly being wielded as political weapons, incentivizing consumers to buy local but also raising the spectre of a trade war that could tip the global economy into a nosedive. A seemingly never-ending series of supposed hundred-year natural disasters have insurance companies so worried that some have withdrawn coverage from vulnerable businesses and households, or pushed premiums to unaffordable levels.

Crises such as the wars in Ukraine and the Middle East would have seemed beyond the sphere of most boards' interest just a few years ago. But they will by no means be the last. The roles of the US, China, India, and Russia in world affairs will surely disrupt corporate planning and decision-making for years to come. Other influential players are also sure to emerge. Take Nigeria, whose population, already over

220 million, is expected to grow to almost 330 million by 2040, not far short of the number currently living in the US. Demographic shifts, whether caused by wars, droughts, sea-level changes, movements from rural to urban areas, or higher levels of education, hold important implications for businesses and their boards.

The board of the future will need to learn that seemingly improbable events can, and surely will, have a big impact on its company's business. It will have to connect the freak summer storms that delay thousands of flights on a midweek afternoon with the resulting loss of productivity in offices, warehouses, and factories because people cannot get to where they planned to go.

And then there is climate change. Johan Rockström and his colleagues at Germany's Potsdam Institute for Climate Impact Research have estimated that climate change will reduce global income by about 19 percent in the twenty-five years between 2024 and 2049 compared to a world that is not warming.[11] By 2049 the cost will be about US$38 trillion a year (well above the output of the entire US economy in 2024), with the poorest regions of the world and those least responsible for heating the atmosphere taking the biggest hit. In the US, the National Climate Assessment estimates that, unless action is taken, climate change will cost the economy up to US$500 billion a year (roughly equal to the current GDP of Thailand) by the end of the century, without counting its enormous toll on human health.[12] Board members will have to fathom that civil unrest triggered by shrivelled crops, water shortages, extreme heat, and widening income inequality eventually translates into supply-chain disruptions and higher costs.

These costs will land on all of us, denting our standard of living, damaging our health, eating into corporate profits, and changing the products and services we consume. The viability of entire industries—among them, tourism, commercial fishing, insurance, and beverage processing—is in jeopardy, along with the tens of millions of people they support. The question is how long businesses can afford to wait before overhauling their products, services, and business models.

It will not be long before today's children are old enough to vote. They may come of age in a world no longer filled with choice and prosperity but spoiled by pollution, inequality, anger, and despair. The sooner the boardroom of today can make the leap to the boardroom of the future, the greater our chances of maintaining their love and respect.

Humanity will also be looking to business to come up with the innovative technologies that can slow down the heating of our planet. Pioneering entrepreneurs and wise corporate leaders have already brought us solar panels and wind turbines, electric vehicles and carbon capture and storage. Beyond providing the talent and imagination to come up with such solutions, business has a crucial role to play in devising the pricing policies, planning regulations, and so forth that will be part of the solution to the climate crisis, thereby ensuring that the planet we call home will remain fit for humanity.

While the changing climate has so far grabbed most of the attention, it is by no means the only nature-related issue that boards of the future must confront. They will have to grapple increasingly with the loss of biodiversity and its costs to their business. The average size of monitored wildlife populations has shrunk by 73 percent since 1970, according to the World

Wildlife Fund's 2024 *Living Planet Report*.[13] Researchers at Queen's University in Belfast have found that populations of almost half of the 70,000 species studied are shrinking, while fewer than three percent are growing.[14]

David Craig, co-chair of the Taskforce on Nature-related Financial Disclosures (TNFD), emphasizes that climate change and nature loss are two sides of the same coin and that companies need to integrate their climate and nature teams to address combined risks and opportunities. He notes that separating climate and nature into different frameworks, like the Task Force on Climate-related Financial Disclosures and the Taskforce on Nature-related Financial Disclosures, is an artificial distinction, and that they should be combined into one framework. Craig also highlights the growing systemic risk from the accumulating "debt" of exploiting natural resources without paying for their use. This trend will eventually lead to ecosystem catastrophes that disrupt business models. He urges boards to fully integrate nature-related issues into their core business strategies to ensure long-term resilience and sustainability.

POLITICS CAN'T BE IGNORED

Much as some business leaders may wish to stay above the nastiness and polarization that now often define the political landscape, they ignore recent developments at their peril. The rise of populism combined with the spread of autocratic rule around the world threatens to upend long-established political systems and erode the stability and predictability that every business craves.

Corporate boards now have little choice but to adapt to the complexities of a world where a business is expected not only to deliver results but also to remain in step with fast-changing expectations and competing interests while staying true to its values. That challenge was encapsulated in 2023 by the experience of the world's number-one brewer, AB InBev, which found itself engulfed by a firestorm after its Bud Light brand partnered with transgender influencer Dylan Mulvaney. Before long, Bud Light had become the target of a consumer boycott and lost its crown as the US's top-selling beer. The parent company's US revenues sank 10.5 percent in the second quarter of 2023 from a year earlier. To make matters worse, it then reversed course, managing to also alienate the LGBTQ+ community.

Every company and its board should be prepared to navigate similar storms in coming years. One way or another, remaining on the sidelines is no longer an option. Rather, each board needs to discuss what values it seeks to uphold for the company it serves, and what action it commits to take—or not take—in the event those values are put to the test. Any board that fails to do this is putting its company at serious risk.

Torben Möger Pedersen, who chairs the Copenhagen Business School and serves on several boards, notes that the world where markets take precedence over politics no longer exists. Now, politics is all too often in the driver's seat, as evidenced by active industrial policies such as the Biden administration's Inflation Reduction Act in the US and moves by European countries to reconfigure their energy supplies in the wake of Russia's invasion of Ukraine. We can undoubtedly expect more such moves under the second Trump administration.

"As a company, you have to accept that," says Möger Pedersen. "See it as a new condition and try to identify the opportunities which arise in this new environment."

BOARDS MUST TAKE NOTICE—AND ACT

Once such new opportunities and threats have been identified, the board must not hesitate to act. To use an admittedly extreme analogy, if a family realizes that the house they live in will be bounded in a year or two by an airport on one side and a highway on the other, does it make sense to talk about what to grow in the garden next summer?

As Martin Wolf put it to me, it is in every corporation's best interest for the board to know which way the wind is blowing:

> Of course, businesses have to pursue their own interests, but they have to be aware, particularly the more important the business is, of its impacts on the context in which they are operating. [Directors] are political actors, because we are all political actors. They're just more important than others. They shouldn't pretend they're not.
>
> It means genuinely trying to help people hit by immense shocks, and I think we haven't done a very good job of that recently. We have to be absolutely committed to equality of opportunity and education, and to getting people good jobs in the society as a whole. And we have to make people feel that they're not constantly getting beaten up by changes in the economy over which they have no control.
>
> Business plays a very big role in this in terms of the sort of jobs it gives people, the sort of economic opportunities it gives, and the sort of policies it supports. Is it just asking

for favours for itself in a rather cynical way and using its resources to weaken regulation where it's necessary? Or is it actually trying to promote some sense of a common weal?

Various labels have emerged to describe this evolving role, among them, inclusive capitalism, stakeholder capitalism, the regenerative economy, the just transition, and the circular economy. The common thread through all these concepts is the ability of a business, through thick and thin, to remain true to its purpose and its values and be sustainable in all its forms.

"Whether you're talking about ESG [environmental, social, and governance] issues or SDGs [the United Nations' sustainable development goals] or about stakeholder capitalism or about inclusive capitalism, all of it is just good business," explains Meredith Sumpter, former chief executive of the Council for Inclusive Capitalism, whose members include leaders of companies large and small around the world. "You're capitalist, so you're pursuing profit," Sumpter adds. "But when you incorporate ESG considerations into your business operations or your investment strategies, you're actually producing a broader kind of value and greatly amplifying the value that a company is capable of producing."

A commitment to sustainability means that boards will have to take a much broader view of "value creation" than in the past. Their success will increasingly be judged not by ups and downs in the share price but by the value that the board and the company it serves bring to those who depend on the business for their well-being—employees, customers, suppliers, and, yes, even people who have no direct dealings with the business but whose lives are affected by its operations.

Maali Khader, chief executive of the Middle East Institute of Directors in Dubai, puts it this way: "When you talk about governance, it's never just the board. You have the board, you have the government, you have the consumer, you have the employees. You need all these stakeholders from all of these directions to come together to get governance to where it needs to be to create the value needed."

Board members who fail to move with the times under their own steam are likely to find themselves being pushed forward—and sometimes backward—by activists, politicians, financial backers, insurance companies, the courts, their own shareholders and employees, and even their own children. These groups may well have different, even contradictory, goals, but the job of a board is to decide which course is in the best interests of its company, and then stick with it.

In particular, let's not forget the growing importance of young people who already spearhead many activist movements and whose voices are sure to grow louder in the years ahead. Increasingly, we can expect to hear the question: Is this the world that we want to inherit from our parents and grandparents?

Thus, no director can afford to ignore the slew of climate-related lawsuits that seek to push governments—and thus inexorably businesses—to take stronger action against global warming. About 230 such actions were filed between 2015 and 2024, more than two-thirds of them after 2020, according to researchers at the London School of Economics.[15] (The study defines these cases as examples of strategic litigation that appears to seek to advance a broader climate action agenda.)

In July 2023, a court in the US state of Montana gave us a taste of what's to come when it ruled in favour of a group of young people demanding that officials must consider climate change when reviewing applications for fossil fuel projects. The verdict was doubly significant given that coal generates about one-third of Montana's energy supplies. The state's supreme court upheld the ruling in December 2024, affirming that the young plaintiffs had a "fundamental constitutional right to a clean and healthful environment." It noted that greenhouse gas emissions have specific effects within the state, "drastically altering and degrading Montana's climate, rivers, lakes, groundwater, atmospheric waters, forests, glaciers, fish, wildlife, air quality, and ecosystem."[17]

In another landmark lawsuit on the other side of the Atlantic, initiated by a group of elderly women, the European Court of Human Rights ruled in April 2024 that the Swiss government had violated its citizens' human rights by not doing enough to halt climate change.[18] Similar cases are being brought with growing frequency by states, cities, and individuals against companies that have allegedly contributed to global warming and failed to protect humanity from its consequences. The most prominent targets so far have been oil and gas giants such as BP, Chevron, ExxonMobil, and Royal Dutch Shell, but there is little doubt that companies in many other sectors will soon find themselves in the crosshairs. Banks and other financial backers are ever more concerned about the rising risk of losses on assets stranded by climate change. Insurers are increasingly struggling to set policy premiums due to the unpredictability of the weather and the damage that it may cause. Importantly, boards need to realize that these developments are unlikely to be reversed by the arrival of a new administration in Washington, DC, or anywhere else for that matter.

REGULATORS ARE NOT SITTING STILL

The rising clamour for improved corporate governance is evident in an array of initiatives around the world. Although efforts are afoot in some countries, notably the US, to turn back the clock, the pace of change has not slowed in Europe and especially not in Asia. Government regulators are paying ever-closer attention to such matters as board oversight, corporate transparency, and the quality of reporting. Likewise, a host of non-governmental organizations continue to formulate new standards, many of them transcending national borders, that will make boards and their companies more accountable to their stakeholders. It is in every board's interest to stay abreast of these initiatives and, where possible, get ahead of them.

Fully half of respondents to the Competent Boards future board survey believe that boards will be under more intense regulatory scrutiny in the future. Thus, when the European Union unveiled plans in November 2024 to consolidate overlapping sustainability rules into a single "omnibus regulation," European Commission president Ursula von der Leyen stressed that the move would not dilute companies' substantive reporting obligations. The focus, she insisted, was to streamline processes, not lower standards.[19]

"The speed of change in the regulatory landscape, as well as the increasing demand by investors, banks, customers, and current and future employees, are really becoming very overwhelming," says Agnes Tai, a Hong Kong–based sustainability investor and climate action influencer.

Below is a brief sampling of the fast-moving and ever-changing regulations and standards around the world that are putting transparency, accountability, and sustainability firmly on board agendas:

- Global disclosure standards are becoming a real game-changer in corporate governance, giving stakeholders a shared vocabulary to evaluate and compare companies' performance. The International Sustainability Standards Board issued its inaugural guidelines in June 2023. Known as IFRS S1 and IFRS S2, the new standards create a common language for investors to assess the impact of sustainability (S1) and climate-related (S2) risks and opportunities on any company's future prospects, no matter where in the world it does business.[20] The standards also require disclosure of the sustainability and climate competencies of the board and senior management. More such standards are in the pipeline covering, for example, nature and biodiversity, human rights, and human capital.

- As of November 2024, thirty jurisdictions had decided to use or were taking steps to introduce the International Sustainability Standards Board guidelines in their legal or regulatory frameworks. Together, they represent about 57 percent of global GDP, more than 40 percent of global market capitalization, and more than half of global greenhouse gas emissions.[21]

- The European Financial Reporting Advisory Group, commonly known as EFRAG, is emerging as one of the most active drivers of change in the field of sustainability reporting. Among the projects it was tackling in early 2025 was an initiative to ensure that financial statements faithfully represent the effects of a company's contracts covering nature-dependent sources of electricity, such as wind and solar.[22] In a sign of its international reach, EFRAG has also taken on the task of drafting sustainability standards for non-EU-based businesses operating in the European Union. The new guidelines, expected to take effect in 2028, will require companies to disclose their greenhouse gas emissions and other climate-related actions.[23]

- Perhaps the most aggressive move so far has come from France, where a "duty of vigilance" law has put some of the country's largest businesses on the defensive.[24] Any firm with more than five thousand employees must now publish an annual "vigilance plan" setting out measures to identify risks and prevent severe impacts on the environment and human rights stemming from its own activities, as well as those of subcontractors and suppliers. Besides a detailed outline of risks and specific actions to mitigate those risks or prevent severe impacts, the company must set up an alert mechanism and a system to monitor the effectiveness of its actions.

- While the second Trump administration has signalled a determination to loosen regulations across a broad swath of the US economy, the drive towards improved governance has by no means run out of steam. California, often the trendsetter for the rest of the country, has adopted a groundbreaking climate disclosure law that is expected to cover about a quarter of the entire US economy, thus significantly influencing corporate governance and sustainability practices nationwide, no matter what the political leanings of the federal government.[25]

The new rules, due to come into force in January 2026, mandate that all large companies doing business in California, including those headquartered outside the state, must disclose their climate-related risks and mitigation strategies. Besides emissions reporting, the law requires companies to disclose their climate risk management strategies, including scenario analyses and the use of internal carbon pricing.

- China introduced its first corporate sustainability disclosure standards in December 2024 aimed at standardizing ESG reporting nationwide and aligning with global reporting frameworks. Under the new rules, ESG reporting will be mandatory for large listed companies starting in 2026, with full implementation by 2030.[26]

- Malaysia, Singapore, and Hong Kong, among others, require directors of publicly listed companies to complete a training program covering key areas such as climate risk management, sustainable business practices, and the integration of environmental considerations into corporate strategy.[27] The Singapore Exchange has published a list of twenty-seven core ESG measurements to help listed companies align their disclosures with international standards. It has also set up a sustainability reporting advisory committee to look at a potential reporting regime for all companies—private as well as public—operating in the country.

- In Latin America, Colombia's stock exchange has collaborated with the Global Reporting Initiative to launch a guide for the preparation of ESG reports. Chile's Financial Market Commission requires certain issuers to disclose their sustainability and corporate governance performances. And Brazil has unveiled plans to integrate the International Financial Reporting Standards (IFRS) sustainability disclosure standards into its own regulatory framework, with mandatory implementation by January 2026.[28]

- It's the same story in the Middle East, where interest in sustainability has grown since the United Arab Emirates played host to the COP28 climate conference in December 2023. Green bond issuance and sustainable finance have shown impressive growth, and there is a trend towards more mandatory reporting on environmental, social and governance matters, according to the Norton Rose Fulbright law firm.[29] The UAE and Saudi Arabia have been especially proactive in enacting new rules. The UAE's Securities and Commodities Authority introduced significant changes to its corporate governance code in 2024, including a requirement that a majority of board members should be non-executive and a third of them independent.[30] The code now also calls for companies to compile an "integrated report" covering its board report, auditor's report, annual financial data, governance reports, and a report by its Sharia control committee.

- In Africa, the Johannesburg Stock Exchange, the continent's largest, published guidelines for listed companies' disclosure of sustainability and climate-change issues in June 2022.[31] "Climate change is a mega-trend impacting all sectors of the economy," the exchange noted. "Therefore, we aim to guide our issuers and investors on understanding the climate crisis and how disclosure can be used not only to anticipate risk, but also to identify opportunities."

How these new disclosure and governance requirements evolve, or how strictly they are enforced, will determine how many businesses comply. Tough business conditions and the rise of populist ideologies have undoubtedly dampened enthusiasm among politicians and business leaders for more regulation. But the fact remains that the environmental activists and community leaders whom boards could once afford to keep at a distance will not melt away. They are still able to raise substantial amounts of money to pursue their causes and, in many cases, have acquired highly effective lobbying and communication skills. The same can be said about those who are against the requirements. However, most agree that we all would like to live in a world with clean water and air.

To board members worried that their companies do not have the financial or human resources to implement this array of initiatives, I have a word of advice: Relax—but get on with it! While some activists may be pushing hard on the accelerator, regulators are aware that compliance takes time. "There is no expectation that every company has to be perfect in its reporting from day one," says Jingdong Hua, the International Sustainability Standards Board's vice-chair. "It's not about being perfect. It's about an endeavour to start good reporting and improvement during the process." Hua adds:

> Our IFRS S2 Climate-Related Disclosures provides a very organized way to guide the board, in terms of how you go about analyzing them from governance, to your strategy, to the identification of key risks and opportunities, and setting up the matrix and targets to guide the delivery of action plans.
>
> Now we have a globally aligned, methodical way of guiding the board so the board can guide management. Disclosure is only the outside part of it. There are also the internal activities, the internal brainstorming, the internal action plans that will produce beneficial results in creating value, in maintaining access to financial resources, reducing costs and financial risks. We keep saying that a company should look at its short-, medium-, and long-term risk and opportunity. Depending on the nature of the business, we leave it to the company and its auditors to define what is short, medium, and long term.
>
> Sustainability is about balancing your current objectives versus long-term objectives. Don't view our standard as a compliance exercise. It's actually enabling the company to think about how it stays a long-term going concern.

Michael Treschow, former chair of the Anglo-Dutch consumer products group Unilever and one of Sweden's most prominent business leaders, urges boards to set priorities but to be flexible:

> I think you need to try not to be too sophisticated. What are the three most important priorities for my company right now that impact us the most? It needs to be business focused. Are we prepared for inflation in the sense that we're not caught with the extra costs without increasing prices? Are we caught in the pandemic which means that everything is closed down? Is it the war in Ukraine? Well, if that's the biggest impact for my company right now, that's what I need to address.
>
> It also depends on what type of business you're in. Maybe you're mostly affected by political happenings because you're so global. Or are you just serving the food market, or whatever? And you need to have a perspective of three, five, or ten years. What are the early warning signs [which determine] what we should do and when we should do it? What are the key performance indicators? The best thing you can do is to have the best people in all your positions. If you do nothing else, spend time on that.

THE COST OF BACKSLIDING

The election of Donald Trump, the ESG/DEI backlash, and the prospect of looser regulation are bound to give many businesses pause, especially in the US. In the current climate, boards are understandably asking whether the continued pursuit of sustainability will bring more costs than benefits. Dare they risk offending powerful politicians, both national and local, by keeping such policies in place? Are their workers and surrounding communities less sympathetic to such initiatives than they might have thought?

Such doubts may be understandable in the short term, but boards that choose to water down or abandon their commitment to sustainability policies risk costly long-term consequences. Whichever way the political winds may be blowing today, the future damage from climate change and nature loss remains frighteningly real. Backtracking from sustainability policies not only risks perpetuating inequalities in society as a whole but tarnishing a company's innovation power as well as its reputation as an enlightened employer.

Paul Polman, former Unilever CEO and chair of the International Chamber of Commerce, puts it this way:

> A good board is a board that takes responsibility for its total impact in the world. A good board ensures that targets are set in line with what the world needs. A good board ensures that companies are proactively implementing things instead of being forced by legislation. A good board runs the business for multiple stakeholders for the longer term.
>
> A good board wants to be sure that the company walks the walk, but also talks the talk.

Let's not forget that many of the world's major economies continue to press ahead with environmental and social initiatives. More than half of the cars sold in China are now electric and hybrid models.[32] The response to France's duty of vigilance law shows that outside stakeholders have little hesitation these days in launching damaging public-relations campaigns and time-consuming lawsuits. A review of over ten thousand ESG-related disputes by Clarity AI, a sustainability technology platform, found that the companies accused of wrongdoing, whether rightly or wrongly, typically suffered a 2–5 percent drop in their share price.[33] "Investors perceive these controversial incidents as a potential sign of poor management or a lack of ethics," the survey concluded, adding that "the growing legal and regulatory consequences of ESG-related incidents can be expensive and time-consuming to resolve as well as reputationally damaging."[34]

The discussion above may leave the impression that anyone signing up for duty on a corporate board is in for a miserable time, weighed down by ever bulkier briefing materials, buffeted between competing interests, and pilloried in public like an unpopular politician. That should not be the case, however, for any directors doing their job properly. The era now dawning over corporate boardrooms is bound to open up exciting new horizons for those with the determination and flexibility to adjust. Artificial intelligence and quantum computing, used properly, could make boards vastly more productive. Innovations spawned by the "green" economy will be augmented by growing attention to the "blue" economy, or the sustainable use of marine resources for economic growth. And much more.

"These are things which are great opportunities for businesses," says Jane Diplock, supervisory board member of the World Benchmarking Alliance and a former director of the Singapore Exchange. The board of the future, Diplock adds, "will need people who will not only understand these opportunities but positively embrace them with enthusiasm, bringing information and knowledge and experience to them to enable them to be successful."

In the chapters that follow, we'll examine how directors can best respond to these seismic shifts in what for many decades has been a stuffy, slow-moving environment. Given the momentous changes taking place outside the boardroom, it would be surprising if some equally dramatic adjustments were not in store for boards themselves. The skills required to be an effective director in the twenty-first century, the composition and role of board committees, the role of the board chair, the adoption of new technologies, relations with a widening array of stakeholders—all these, and more, are set to change dramatically in the years ahead.

Suffice to say for now that the boardroom of the future will have no choice but to embrace change and gird for the challenges ahead. As I see it, board members will be more willing than their predecessors to listen, more willing to learn, more willing to collaborate, and more willing to take a broader view of their responsibilities. Some current board members may even have to admit that they are no longer as well equipped for the job as they once were or ought to be. The time may have come for them to step aside so that a new generation can seize the moment.

///

Ten Questions for the Board of the Future

1. How is your board ensuring that the organization remains resilient and adaptive to rapidly shifting stakeholder expectations, technological advancements, and geopolitical tensions while maintaining a consistent strategic vision?

2. What governance structures or practices have you implemented to balance short-term agility with long-term accountability?

3. What are the top three trends—social, economic, environmental, technological, or geopolitical—that your board believes will fundamentally reshape its industry over the next three, five, and ten years?

4. What systemic risks (e.g., cyberattacks, climate shocks, nature loss, AI disruptions) has your board prioritized for scenario planning, and how are you integrating these risks into strategic decision-making?

5. What are the three most significant existential risks these trends pose to your company, and how is the board preparing for them?

6. Can your board identify three untapped opportunities stemming from these same developments, and how is it mobilizing to capture them?

7. How does your board ensure that decision-making is informed by diverse sources and perspectives, avoiding echo chambers or confirmation bias?

8. What tools, partnerships, or advisory channels is your board using to stay ahead of emerging legislation and evolving regulatory landscapes, including mandatory climate-, nature-, or AI-related disclosures?

9. Can you recall a recent scenario where your board's collective thinking or strategic direction shifted significantly after incorporating diverse data points or stakeholder feedback? What drove that shift?

10. How has your boardroom culture and operational approach evolved in the past five years to align with the complexities of a digital, decentralized, and sustainability-conscious economy? What practices or innovations are you most proud of?

CHAPTER TWO

Wanted: A Fresh Approach

Every company has to be thinking about where they need to be a little bit ahead of where society is, but not so far ahead that they get killed.

—Chad Holliday, former chairman of Royal Dutch Shell and Bank of America

A board's job is infinitely more difficult than it was just a few years ago. Directors face a slew of new obstacles, from regulatory complexities and the challenges of dealing with an ever-widening array of activists, to the heightened risk of lawsuits and multiplying demands on their time. If we're honest, however, we need to acknowledge that some of the blame for this state of affairs rests with boards themselves.

While the external environment has undoubtedly become more complicated, many, if not most, directors have been far too slow in responding to the fast-moving world around them. From the way directors are recruited to how they perform their roles, many boards continue to adhere to outdated and increasingly ineffective practices. For instance, companies often select board members based solely on their expertise in a specific field or business area. However, as Eric Wetlaufer, former head of the CPP Investment Board's public markets investment department, observes, "The experience these directors rely upon is often rooted in a distant past that becomes less relevant with each passing day."

Governance experts are increasingly advising companies to turn to wise generalists with a broader view of the wide-ranging issues that boards face today. Chad Holliday reckons that no more than two or three members of a board need to have deep knowledge of the sector in which their company operates. Almost two-thirds of respondents to the Competent Boards future boardroom survey take the view that interpersonal skills, such as emotional intelligence, adaptability, and critical strategic thinking, will be the most important attributes of board members in an era dominated by artificial intelligence. Given this evolution, boards and those who serve on them will need to change the way they approach their duties. This chapter outlines some of the ways in which the transition may unfold.

OUTCOMES-BASED GOVERNANCE

For decades, a board was considered to be doing its job if it set up efficient processes and control systems, and then ensured that management adhered to them. The problem is that a set of reporting requirements, even if they are rigidly followed, may give few clues to success or failure. "I'm really concerned that ESG reporting metrics are all process and output based," says Tensie Whelan, director of New York University's Stern Center for Sustainable Business. "They're not performance based. Basically, we're seeing the tail wag the dog. People are just, 'Okay, I need to report. What are some data I can get to report? Okay, good, I'm done.'"

The good news is that old habits are starting to die. Increasingly, boards are being urged to put the emphasis on results and performance, a system known as outcomes-based governance. This emphasis on outcomes concentrates the board's mind on achievement (and, for that matter, failure) rather than process. Whelan gives this example to illustrate the difference:

> Let's say you're an apparel company, and you're asked if you have a chemical management policy. What does that mean? Yes, I do. Okay, fine. But that means there's no difference in the reporting metrics between a company that has a reporting policy on chemicals versus a company that has developed a bio-based dye that reduces chemicals, water use, and energy use. The second company is creating operational efficiencies and something that's going to drive customer demand.
>
> Which one is going to make you money? Which is going to reduce your risk? Just having a chemical management policy is going to do absolutely nothing for you, whereas having an innovative bio-based product could really do a lot for you. If you're just going to tick the box on all this stuff, you're not going to drive improvement for society and you're not going to drive improvement for yourself. It's just going to be a cost centre, because you're just going to be reporting, and that costs money. Why not devise a strategy that's going to drive better performance?

Whelan is spot on—which is why we need competent boards that can ask the right questions and know what answers they are looking for. Not a checking-the-box exercise, but a strategy. By measuring accomplishments against the goals that were set, outcomes-based governance strengthens responsibility and accountability, both for management and for the board itself.

Knowing the expected outcomes from a particular initiative or project also helps directors ask the right questions. "For good board governance, it's a question of questions," says Erika Karp, executive director of the Aspen Institute's Finance Leaders Fellowship. "Board members need to think of themselves as constantly questioning in just the same way as they're thinking of constant renewal."

Comparing outcomes with goals should be on the agenda of every board meeting. While it's impractical for a board to review every outcome against goals at each meeting, it can focus on key priorities by using dashboards that summarize critical metrics, delegating detailed reviews to committees, and scheduling deep dives quarterly or biannually. Regular updates should highlight significant deviations or risks to strategic objectives, ensuring discussions remain targeted, forward looking, and impactful without overloading the agenda. Without such a discussion, the risk is that the board will only consider the financial results of the company's actions, rather than gaining a full picture of the business's impact on the world around it.

Writing in the *Financial Times* a few years ago, the veteran South African corporate governance expert Mervyn King listed four critical outcomes that stakeholders should push corporate boards to aim for: first, ethical cultures with effective leadership; second, trust and confidence in the company among the communities where it operates; third, adequate and effective risk controls; and, finally, the ability to create value in a sustainable manner. "If stakeholders' rational conclusion is that a company is achieving those four outcomes, the company can be said to be practising quality governance," King observed.[35]

DEFINE YOUR BOARD'S PURPOSE

It is no longer enough for a board to set out a vision or mission statement, or a list of "strategic objectives." As Mervyn King puts it, once a board accepts that its company has a goal beyond delivering a return to the providers of capital, "it has to sit down and really think about: What is the purpose of this business?"

That exercise should start with the board examining its own purpose and the purpose of its individual members, given that they are collectively the company's top decision-making authority. In other words, a purpose-driven mindset must be the hallmark of a future-prepared board member.

Pat Gallardo Dwyer, founder of the Purpose Business based in Hong Kong and Singapore, observes that "clarity and activation of organizational purpose allow businesses to deliver on the well-being of all people and the planet. When your role and impact are clear and you deliver on them consistently, profitability becomes an engine that drives responsible business practices—a means to an end, not the end itself."

In my mind, a good starting point in defining the board's purpose is to ask a number of seemingly simple but probing questions. Here are some of my favourites:

- What is our role as the board? What are we as individuals and as a board here to do? What are our ethical responsibilities?

- What value have we brought to the company as individuals and as the board the past year? What value do we hope to bring in the year(s) to come?

- What do management, investors, suppliers, employees, customers, and other stakeholders expect from us, both generally and in specific situations? Did we deliver on the expectations? Why/why not? How did we do it? Can we learn from the process?

- Likewise, what will these stakeholders expect of us in two, five, or ten years?

- How can we, both collectively and individually, be of service to the company so that we leave it in a better place than when we joined the board?

- Do we agree on how our business creates value beyond financial returns?

- What fundamental problem are we solving, or need are we fulfilling, for our stakeholders? Does all our communication reflect this?

- What are the principles or values that have defined our company historically, and how should they evolve to meet future challenges and opportunities?

- What would our stakeholders lose if this company no longer existed?

- What or who could 'kill' this company?

- Do we agree on a communication defining the board's purpose?

The answers to these questions should provide some valuable clues about board members' values, their strengths and weaknesses, and the dynamics around the boardroom table. They will tell us who is attuned to swift decision-making and decisive action, and who are the long-term thinkers. They should also reveal who has the courage to ask tough questions and who will speak up if the company is straying from ethical behaviour, or if there is a risk of resources being wasted on projects not aligned with the company's mission.

The board has a responsibility to ensure that the many interests that go into defining the company's purpose have a reasonable chance of producing long-term success. It must be able to show that while it may not be able to give every group of stakeholders everything they want, it is striving for a broader social purpose that goes beyond a quarterly earnings target. A statement of purpose might thus include references to such issues as climate change, nature and biodiversity protection and regeneration, sustainability in general, human rights, corporate citizenship, labour relations, and lobbying policies. In short, it should tell us how the board will make the world a better place for those who depend on the business for their livelihoods.

Erika Karp describes how the various strands of sustainability are interwoven and cannot be tackled without an overall sense of purpose:

Let's assume my company is working to give the world access to financial services, to water, to health care, to energy, with access as the single common denominator. The United Nations' sustainable development goals are all interrelated. You can't give the world access to gender equity unless you give women access to water and health care and capital and broadband. As a board member, I want to see my company contribute to the creation of access to these things. And then you have purpose.

HOW TO PREPARE FOR THE FUTURE

In a fast-paced environment with many unknowns, board members need to have qualities and skills that have been given far too little attention in the past. The board is expected to not only evaluate the current landscape but also learn to project its wisdom beyond what is visible so that it can identify fresh—and perhaps even surprising—opportunities and alert management to impending risks.

A key attribute of future-ready board members is that they have acquired their wisdom through a deep-rooted sense of curiosity and a willingness to learn. They are willing to adjust their views by listening to stakeholders with diverse and even contrary opinions. They recognize the interconnectivity of the various elements of our society and are committed to finding solutions that meet the needs of a wide variety of stakeholders.

TURNING HINDU PHILOSOPHY INTO BOARDROOM PRACTICE

What is the purpose of the board? Any aspiring board member would do well to embrace four qualities inspired by the Vedanta philosophical tradition, according to retired Tata Sons executive director R. Gopalakrishnan:

- Heightened self-awareness. Ask yourself: Who am I? Why am I here? What is my deeper purpose?

- An eagerness to protect resources, whether they be people, animals and plants, water, electricity ... and many more.

- An awareness that service to other people is more important than service to yourself.

- An ability to take decisions ruthlessly but to execute them with compassion.

Shailesh Haribhakti, an independent director of companies in the Holcim Group, puts it this way: "Like a stately person who cares for the environment, social issues, and governance in a strategic sense, this person should possess moral, domain knowledge, intellectual, and spiritual capital, and must be ready to deploy all these capitals fearlessly."

Successful board members play an essential role in distilling their company's purpose into a vision that also reflects society's shared principles and values. They have an ability to communicate how board-level actions align with the long-term interests of the company, and they foster the entrepreneurial spirit that drives a compelling strategic vision.

Honesty plays a key role in gaining trust with fellow board members, senior management, and outside stakeholders. Therefore, future-ready board members must be transparent when engaging in cooperative processes and remain account-able to the stated purpose and given strategy. Establishing a boardroom culture of respect and transparency encourages innovation by creating a space where honest opinions can be shared without hesitation. Such a mindset welcomes conflict-ing arguments that, in turn, shape direction and ultimately produce a powerful shared vision.

Board members should be willing not only to express their own opinions but to engage with others in order to avoid groupthink, a common failing of many boards. Future-ready board members will have to be forthright and precise in their questioning.

Board members should view diversity of thought as an opportunity to engage with new ideas and where necessary to challenge the status quo, even if this causes some discomfort. According to a PwC corporate directors survey, 17 percent of directors find it difficult to challenge the status quo or voice a dissenting opinion.[36] This hesitation underlines the impor-tance of keeping boardroom discussions open and respectful if the board is to deliver truly insightful and useful ideas.

In today's climate of economic uncertainty and politi-cal polarization, we dare not forfeit the progress that has taken place over the past few decades, nor can we afford to lose sight of the urgency surrounding issues such as the cli-mate crisis, biodiversity loss, and racial injustice. Another essential element of a future-ready board's toolbox is competence in environmental, social, and governance issues. As noted by Jane Diplock, supervisory board member of the World Benchmarking Alliance and a former director of the Singapore Exchange, "Understanding that profitability and performance are interdependent with community expectations of sustainability is a fundamental concern."

Board members should not hesitate to use the tools, resources, and opportunities that can help broaden their understanding of critical environmental, social, and governance topics and how to address them. Thus, while rapid advancements in technology may bring heightened cybersecurity risks, they also open up new avenues for education and learning. Improved availability of information is bound to boost data-driven solutions that ultimately promote sustainable development. It is worth noting, however, that a vast expansion of data will require a vast amount of energy, underlining the correlation between data security and energy security.

A willingness to acquire the knowledge, skills, and confidence to take proactive action on sustainability-related challenges will thus be a key quality of a future-ready board member. Every board's skills matrix should reflect these competencies so stakeholders can evaluate individual directors' preparedness.

Here are some of the traits and competencies discussed in this chapter:

- Strategic foresight and critical thinking

- Assessment of scenario planning

- Curiosity and lifelong learning

- Stakeholder-centric decision-making

- Purpose-driven governance

- Ethical leadership

- Cultural intelligence and diversity of thought

- Innovation and technological literacy

- Decision-making ability under uncertainty

- Accountability and transparency

- Environmental and social stewardship

- Resilience and adaptability

It may not be practical to include every competency in a published skills matrix, especially since many are difficult to measure. Instead, board members can use their own internal assessments to rate themselves and their peers on key competencies. This may involve prioritizing specific skills and using a simple scoring system (for example, rating from 1 to 10), rather than vague options like Yes/No or Always/Mostly/ Never, which often lack depth. Looking ahead, external board assessors are likely to play a role in this process by "signing off" on board assessment statements in much the same way as auditors vouch for financial statements.

SOFT SKILLS TO THE FORE

Directors of the future are unlikely to act differently from their predecessors if they do not think differently. One way of making that happen is through the recruitment process. In the search for new members, we can expect that the board of the future will put more emphasis on "soft" skills.

"We need people in the boardroom who can anticipate and deal with turbulence and uncertainty at levels which are far higher than what people have experienced in the last forty or fifty years," says Anirban Ghosh, former chief sustainability officer of India's Mahindra Group. Carolynn Chalmers, chief executive of the Good Governance Academy, adds: "The future boardroom needs to be equipped to govern rapid change impacting the whole organization."

While board members are expected to bring an array of formal skills to the table, their effectiveness will increasingly be measured in the future by their character or, to put it another way, how their inner compass guides their decisions. "Good governance depends on good behaviour," says R. Gopalakrishnan, a retired director of India's Tata Sons conglomerate. "Governance sounds legalistic and bureaucratic, but it is an entirely human activity."

Inclusiveness is another essential trait for board members in the twenty-first century. If directors are to properly serve the communities in which their company operates, they must have perspectives and lived experiences that reflect those communities. Thus, they should spare no effort to tap into dimensions of diversity and encourage perspectives that may not have existed previously. In short, they must be citizens of the world rather than representatives of a single country or culture.

Courage, empathy, and persuasiveness undoubtedly help promote the dialogue that leads to better decision-making. They underscore the importance of approaching challenges and even failures with an entrepreneurial mindset. That includes a penchant for creative problem-solving in times of uncertainty when no playbook exists. Add to those the curiosity that helps a board identify novel solutions in the drive for innovation. A company whose board embraces curiosity, seeks out new opportunities, and then has the courage to act on them is far more likely to keep moving forward even in the toughest times.

In my get-togethers with Competent Boards network, I often ask which personal traits they think will be most in demand from future board members. Over and over, the answer is the same: curiosity, an inquiring mind, and foresight. Mervyn King bluntly sums up what boards should be looking for: "You need a person who's not afraid to say: 'I don't understand this report. Could the chief executive please explain to me what is on page five? What does this mean? Because as I read it, it says this and this. Is that what you intended?'"

Joyce Cacho, an independent director and chair of Sistema Biobolsa, adds an insightful nuance: "By curiosity, I don't mean voyeurism. I mean an eagerness to learn and experience, not to judge or to boast about one's experiences."

Of course, the effective director of the future will also possess many other attributes, among them, flexibility, an openness to new ideas, and a nose for the unexpected, whether opportunities or threats. Here is Cacho's take:

> My ideal boardroom is filled with people who are committed to lifelong learning, constantly absorbing new information and perspectives. They need to be thoughtful, with a shared agenda that ensures they won't put their

board colleagues or the company at risk. They should aim
to bring out the best in those they work with. That, to me,
is part of the duty of loyalty.

Kathleen Taylor, chair of Element Fleet Management and
former Royal Bank of Canada chair, stresses the importance of
directors pushing the boundaries of their knowledge not only
in their own companies but in the world around them. "A lot
of times," she says, "if you look at what causes businesses to
fail, it's externalities. It's things they didn't see coming, that
were outside the bounds of the boardroom. So having a management team and directors who can see around corners is
really, really important."

Several members of the Competent Boards network listed
proactive forward thinking near the top of the attributes
likely to be most in demand in the future boardroom.

Jane Diplock says a board member should never stop asking:
"How can we transform our business model into something
which is going to fit this changed landscape that we have in
front of us? And how can we use digital and other tools to
make that happen?" In a similar vein, Maali Khader, chief
executive of the Middle East Institute of Directors, observes
that "you should always be ahead of the curve. If you're
responding to regulation, you're a little behind the curve. If
you have the right practices, you will always go above and
beyond regulatory requirements. Regulations set the minimum standard, and companies should be aspiring to a lot
more than that."

The climate crisis has underscored the urgency of a fresh,
forward-thinking outlook. Every board now needs directors
who appreciate the far-reaching consequences of extreme

weather events for their own industries and companies. As Anirban Ghosh notes:

> If you are in, say, the cement industry, and you don't anticipate the pressures on producing clean cement, whichever company you are guiding is very likely not going to be competitive in the future, because somebody is going to work on a solution. That is the future of the cement industry, as it is for the steel industry and the aluminum industry, and so on. It is so critical for mankind. Likewise, if you're on a board of directors in a business that works with materials or processing materials, and you're not guiding them towards opportunities that are emerging in the circular economy, then it is very likely that your company will miss the next big bus of value creation in material processing.

A TIME FOR REJUVENATION

Corporate directors need to do some serious soul-searching, both individually and collectively, if they are to make a successful transition to the board of the future.

Competition for directorships will intensify as boards reach out to a wider set of demographics and are more open to recruiting generalists rather than specialists. "Today, the perception of a board director is that it's a nice thing to do for any guy who's retiring, and that it adds to my pension," says R. Gopalakrishnan. But, he adds, "the money has to be earned, and it's earned by finding a pathway to being a wise director."

That pathway is likely to include more training and education, with expertise in sustainability becoming an especially valuable attribute. As new regulations and standards come to require disclosure of the board's sustainability and climate competencies, directors will have to demonstrate their knowledge by producing evidence of formal education or professional experience. This could take the form of certifications, degrees, or previous work experience related to sustainability, climate change, biodiversity, nature, and other environmental, social, and governance issues that may be relevant to the company and its stakeholders.

Another practice that will come under growing scrutiny is the long-standing assumption that directors are reappointed year in and year out with few questions asked about their performance. (We examine the issue of diversity in the boardroom of the future in more detail in chapter six.) Likewise, the trend over the past decade or two of separating the positions of chair and chief executive will likely continue amid concerns over whether one person can adequately do both jobs and, more important, whether such an arrangement meets today's standards of accountability.

BLAZING THE WAY TO A NEW APPROACH

The Mission Possible Partnership, set up in 2020, brings together three hundred of the world's most prominent companies, non-governmental organizations, and think-tanks to show that zero-carbon policies can work even in industries where this once seemed impossible. The partnership covers seven sectors that make up 30 percent of global emissions—aluminum, cement, steel, shipping, aviation, trucking, and chemicals.

Chad Holliday, who chairs the partnership, says it seeks to strike a balance so that companies are "a little bit ahead" of society's current norms, but not so far ahead that they risk alienating their shareholders and destroying their business. Thus, a chemicals producer might start off by building just one "green" plant, learn from its experience, and then go on to build more. "We're trying to get investors involved around how they can publicly say 'We think every major chemical company ought to start down (that road), and we will support that,'" says Holliday.

The partnership is run by the World Economic Forum, the Energy Transitions Commission, RMI, and the We Mean Business Coalition.

NATURE'S PLACE AT THE TABLE

One question I often ask Competent Boards network is whether they favour giving "nature" a seat at the boardroom table. The reason I ask is that climate change and the threat to fauna and flora are having an ever more serious impact on every company's business. The World Economic Forum, which can hardly be described as a bunch of tree huggers, has estimated that more than half of the world's GDP is highly or moderately dependent on nature. Global sales of pharmaceuticals based on materials of natural origin are worth an estimated US$75 billion a year, while natural wonders such as coral reefs are essential to food production and tourism. Yet the WEF's 2025 *Global Risks Report* ranks biodiversity loss and ecosystem collapse together as the second biggest global long-term (10 years) risk for humanity.[37]

The responses to my question are invariably illuminating, but by no means identical. Let's start with Mahindra's Anirban Ghosh:

> It is important to bring nature to the table. It is important to have an understanding of the negative impacts. If nature was on the board, and if nature sent us an invoice, most companies would shut down. We've been awfully fortunate that we've had access to natural resources without paying any economic value for them. The cost of extracting petroleum or metals is nowhere near their economic value. And the cost of the pollution that we've caused in the process of extracting materials is something that we've only just started experiencing at scale. This can get a whole lot worse.

Eric Wetlaufer emphasizes that nature's well-being—and the threats to it—should concern us all:

> Nature absolutely deserves a seat at the table. That doesn't necessarily mean having one board member solely dedicated to representing nature, but it does mean recognizing the growing risks and importance of the company's interaction with the natural world. Unfortunately, these issues have often been kept in the background, and it's time we bring them to the forefront.
>
> I often hear pushback on ESG, with the argument that it's not up to businesses to solve these problems. But the

reality is, it's not up to any single entity—it's up to all of us. Everyone has a role to play. Board members in particular have an opportunity to lead, mindful of nature's interests and incorporating those perspectives into their decision-making whenever it's relevant.

Kristjan Jespersen, associate professor and sustainable campus program manager at the Copenhagen Business School, takes a more middle-of-the-road view. While agreeing that nature, whether in the form of biodiversity loss, deforestation, or water impacts, affects every company and its supply chain, he sounds a note of caution:

> Before we rush headlong into saying "Do we need a committee or a focus on nature on the board?" we have to prepare the board to understand the intricacies and the challenges of dealing with nature. There is a risk that the company recognizing these risks moves too quickly. What's then going to happen is that you're going to have the biggest companies successfully cherry-picking and de-risking their supply chains, ensuring that there's no deforestation, while the vast majority of other companies are stuck with complex supply chains with very high rates of deforestation.
>
> We have to be much more aware that nature and people coexist. Instead of just doing a de-risking exercise, we have to start understanding how to embed the cost of nature and conservation finance into the price of our goods. This is going to be a very controversial issue because we have grown comfortable with cheap products.
>
> But if we can understand how to carry those costs of conservation and embed a couple of cents into every KitKat bar or La Mer skin cream or whatever, then we'll be able to

come up with more sustainable solutions. When it comes to nature, it boils down to the board taking a more nuanced approach and a willingness to learn. Nature should not be an add-on, it should not be philanthropy. It should be embedded into the cost of each product and every consumer must cover that cost.

If there is a common thread in these responses, it is that board members and senior managers can no longer ignore nature and its many manifestations in their deliberations. On the plus side, the World Economic Forum has estimated that investing in a nature-positive economy could unlock US$10.1 trillion of business opportunities a year and create 395 million jobs by 2030 through, for example, the use of regenerative agriculture, sustainable forest management, and development of more transparent supply chains. According to the WEF, such actions would help transform our food, infrastructure, and energy supplies, the three systems responsible for almost 80 percent of nature loss.[38]

The Taskforce on Nature-related Financial Disclosures has published a global framework aimed at ensuring that nature is considered alongside other business risks. The seriousness of this initiative was underlined by an opinion issued by two Australian lawyers in November 2023 that company directors can be held personally liable if they fail to foresee the impact that their businesses have on nature and the commercial risks that those effects pose.[39] One example of such a risk is the EU's ban on imports of beef raised on deforested land. According to the Australian lawyers, companies need to disclose the risk that they could lose access to valuable markets if they continue to sell beef linked to deforestation.

The cost to nature will, I believe, become an integral part of the calculation that goes into any corporate project or product. In that sense, nature will indeed have a powerful voice at the boardroom table. Companies can get ahead of the game by including shadow pricing on the resources nature currently delivers for free. Such initiatives are likely to be applauded even if the price point turns out to be wrong or is based on the cost of repairing the harm done by the company and its products.

WHAT TO DO ABOUT NATURE?

When it comes to nature, David Craig has some succinct advice for the board of the future: Stop thinking about nature as a corporate social responsibility, and instead treat it as a core part of your business model and a core investment.

"You can't find a company anywhere in the world or an investment portfolio that isn't dependent on nature in some critical way," says Craig, co-chair of the Taskforce on Nature-related Financial Disclosures and former CEO of Refinitiv, a large provider of financial data and analytics. The taskforce has 1,500 members from over one hundred countries.

According to Craig, the first question that companies concerned about their impact on nature typically ask is: Where are we located? "Every company might know their legal entity, they might know which countries they're in or even the areas they're in," Craig notes. "But they haven't really mapped out the ecosystem that they're in and the impacts or the dependencies."

A board should then be inquiring about supply chains and sensitive ecosystems relevant to its business. "Don't assume it's just about water. It's amazing how many companies have come back and said: 'We thought we were just about water. We now realize we have a major issue on pollination and pollinators or use of plastics.' Then start to work with the supply chain and start looking at alternative ways where pressures can be alleviated."

Craig emphasizes the importance of being proactive. "If you're having the discussion at the tail end, you're missing the opportunity to say, 'Hey, we can change our business model here. We can make the investment up front before it's too late. We can move away from the things that are causing harm that we know we can't continue forever.'"

LOOK BEYOND THE ABBREVIATIONS

The recent backlash against the environmental, social, and governance movement, discussed in more detail in the next chapter, has by no means diminished the responsibilities of a board and its individual directors. On the contrary, it cannot obscure the reality that, while the term environmental, social and governance (ESG) may have become toxic in some quarters, board decisions are increasingly being judged against the yardsticks of sustainability, inclusive capitalism, a just transition ... call it what you will. These concepts are pervading, and will continue to pervade, the board's entire agenda.

As an example of how far the goalposts are moving, Chad Holliday, former chairman of Royal Dutch Shell and Bank of America, points to the implications for a business of poor health-care facilities. "What does it mean for a company if it is going into a developing country that doesn't have vaccines or clean drinking water?" Holliday asks, noting that the answers to such questions will increasingly influence a board's investment decisions. "How do you think about your role there, your responsibilities there? A company has to think about that."

Kristjan Jespersen cautions that sustainability must be more than a reporting tool:

> Companies that stay in the kind of framework where they just do a check-the-boxes exercise are going to be on the back foot in comparison to companies that are leveraging those insights not just for their sustainability office or their reporting tools, but to translate that information into their operations or supply chain management.

Such information can be useful, for example, for ranking suppliers according to their labour practices and human-rights records.

I have no reason to believe that the gains of the past decade will be reversed anytime soon. As FairVote's Meredith Sumpter puts it: "Companies are just beginning to realize what 'just transition' is, that it's the advancement of social in addition to environmental goals." She adds:

> Consumers are expecting greater things from business leaders, whether you're the CEO or whether you're providing

guidance as a board member. And the way that we show up as business leaders and engage the public about the value that we're creating is by tackling these environmental, climate, and inclusivity risks head-on. That is just good business.

Just how nimble companies must be these days was underlined by the brazen murder in December 2024 of the chief executive of UnitedHealthcare, one of the largest health insurers in the US. A poll conducted shortly afterwards by NORC at the University of Chicago put the blame for the attack squarely on the practices of the US healthcare industry.[40] No wonder that the killing sent shivers down the spines of many CEOs and board members, forcing them to confront tough questions not only about their personal security but about their companies' business model, customer service, process, and culture.

Sustaining the needed far-reaching changes in process and culture will not be easy. But the combination of a far-sighted board and careful planning can achieve the best of both worlds—forging ahead with sustainability initiatives without sacrificing short-term profits. Royal Dutch Shell's board sought to do just that by installing electric chargers on the forecourts of its sprawling network of retail gasoline stations, the largest in the world. "We were really helping the electric car owners make that leap and get out in front," recalls Chad Holliday. The chargers initially ran at a loss because they were not used enough. But Shell managed to step up their throughput by revamping and promoting the coffee shops and convenience stores adjacent to the forecourts, thereby tempting motorists to do some shopping while their cars were charging. As Holliday puts it, "We tried to find a way to offset the added cost of the electricity with the retail."

If every board starts thinking that way, business will be able to play a much bigger role in creating a sustainable future for the planet. Andrew Behar, chief executive of As You Sow, a California-based non-profit shareholder representative organization, is among the optimists. "We're seeing that, for the most part, companies actually want to get better," he says. "The boards of directors want to fit into the new paradigm as it reduces risk for all stakeholders and leads to long-term sustainable growth."

III

Ten Questions for the Board of the Future

1. What's the purpose of your board? Are you genuinely driving long-term success or just going through the motions? (See questions on page 32.)

2. Are you stuck in an echo chamber, or do you actively seek out and embrace tough, diverse opinions that challenge your thinking?

3. Are you focused on real results that matter, or are you just ticking boxes and playing it safe?

4. Do you understand the financial and operational risks of ignoring climate, nature, and societal shifts, or are you gambling with the future?

5. Are you listening to your stakeholders or just assuming you know what they want?

6. Are you preparing for what's next, or are you constantly reacting and playing catch-up?

7. Does your board have the skills to tackle the challenges of tomorrow, or is it relying on outdated expertise? When was the last time the board updated its skills matrix?

8. Are you fostering meaningful debate, or is each meeting just a room full of nodding heads?

9. Are you leading with integrity, or prioritizing convenience over doing what's right?

10. Are you creating a company built to last, or just focused on hitting the next quarter's numbers?

CHAPTER THREE

The Shifting Governance Landscape

What comes to bite you is not the thing that is on the board agenda, it's the thing you didn't think of or didn't recognize. What doesn't work is pretending everything is fine or expecting the future to be like the past because it never is. You can't predict the future, but you can prepare for the future.

—*Sarah Keohane Williamson, CEO, FCLTGlobal*

Unfortunately, boards often cannot resist the temptation to chase shiny objects rather than pay attention to long-term trends. Groupthink can discourage and even drown out quiet voices of wisdom around the boardroom table. And the pressures of today often take precedence over the priorities of tomorrow. Nowhere has this behaviour been more apparent than in the discussion of the issues behind the—by now universally known—abbreviations ESG and DEI.

The blowback against ESG (environmental, social, and governance—just in case you've forgotten) and DEI (diversity, equity, and inclusion) has reached fever pitch in recent years, especially in the US. Critics have slammed "woke" corporations for going too far in kowtowing to activists and progressive politicians, instead of being left alone to get on with what, in their judgment, is material and relevant for their businesses.[41]

Much of the backlash has its roots in the "culture wars" that have roiled the US as populist politicians and far-right activists rail against so-called "woke capitalism." The sustainability movement has been caught up in the same highly charged and politically divisive atmosphere that has enveloped reproductive issues, gun control, and racial discrimination. Numerous prominent US financial companies, including BlackRock, Blackstone, Raymond James, and T. Rowe Price, cautioned in their 2023 annual reports that "divergent views" and "competing demands" on ESG investing could damage their financial performance. The *Financial Times* reported that at least a dozen of the biggest American financial services companies warned in their 2023 annual reports that the backlash against sustainable investing had become a material risk to their business.

The chorus of criticism has had tangible consequences. The number of anti-ESG shareholder proposals submitted to US companies shot up from an average of about 20 a year between 2014 and 2020 to 108 in 2024. Fifteen climate-related proposals were submitted in 2024, up from 6 the previous year, while those addressing companies' diversity and equity practices ballooned from 5 to 17, according to the Conference Board.[42] Several Republican-controlled states have blacklisted US and European financial groups that they view as overly hostile to fossil fuels. Texas's exclusion list runs to 10 banks and 348 investment funds.[43] Numerous state legislatures have also passed laws that ban or limit the consideration of environmental, social and governance issues in investment decisions.[44]

BlackRock's chairman and chief executive, Larry Fink, has said that he will no longer use the abbreviation and, sure enough, it has been banished from his annual letter to Black-Rock stakeholders. BlackRock has instead moved towards a broader strategy known as "transition investing" which, among other elements, involves heavy investment in clean-energy projects.[45] Numerous other companies have also stopped using the term ESG in the face of pressure from investors, politicians, and threats of legal action, the *Wall Street Journal* reported.[46]

Lawsuits are piling up. Among them, eleven US states, led by Texas, accused BlackRock and two other prominent investment managers in November 2024 of abusing their shareholdings in major coal producers to coerce the companies to cut production in order to boost returns on the funds' clean-energy investments, resulting in higher energy costs for US consumers.[47] The three money managers have described the allegation as baseless and BlackRock has said that it "defies common sense."

SUSTAINABILITY WILL TRIUMPH

Despite these bumps in the road, I firmly believe that sustainable governance is more crucial than ever for the well-being of companies, and that the sustainability agenda is here to stay. The green transition isn't about quick fixes but about fostering a long-term vision and executing short-term actions that align with that vision. Boards will be instrumental in that process. By equipping themselves with the tools and foresight needed, board members can drive their companies towards responsible and effective action.

For starters, sustainability advocates need to get the message across more forcefully that these concepts are not a call to activism, but rather a valuable framework to identify risks and opportunities with the goal of securing long-term benefits both for the specific business and for humanity as a whole. No company can survive in a world that fails. Critics often fail to understand that.

I am convinced that the backlash against ESG and DEI, like the resistance to corporate social responsibility in the early years of the millennium, will turn out to be transitory. While the abbreviations themselves may have attracted much disdain in recent years, almost everyone, whatever their political persuasion, agrees on the need to confront the very real challenges facing our planet such as polluted air and water, human trafficking, racism, extreme weather events, and corruption.

The board of the future will have no choice but to face up to these realities. They are all material issues that are sure to have an impact on businesses in every sector of the economy and in every part of the world. A board's fiduciary duty of care requires it to recognize these issues, disclose them to everyone with an interest in the business, and then act in a way that makes the situation better, not worse. At the same time, the polarized state of public discourse should encourage boards to be more nimble and more sensitive to the forces swirling around them—which is never a bad thing.

"We are at an inflection point," says As You Sow's Andrew Behar. "You have to decide whether your company is going to join an emerging economy based on justice and sustainability that is going to be thriving into the future. Or you can make a decision to be part of the extractive economy and your company will probably be winding down. Right now, there isn't a middle ground."

I am confident that the board of the future will see sustainability as an integral part of sound business practice. The Danish toymaker LEGO Group is a great example. Any observer might have been forgiven for thinking that the company was backing away from its commitment to make its colourful toy bricks entirely from sustainable materials by 2032 when it announced in September 2023 that it was shelving plans to produce them from recycled plastic bottles made of polyethylene terephthalate (PET). Could LEGO be joining the growing chorus of skepticism about a business model built on sustainability? Had it decided that the costs of a net-zero economy outweighed the benefits? Not at all.

Rather, LEGO had concluded that using PET would do little to reduce its carbon emissions. Far from abandoning the 2032 target, it has insisted that it remains "fully committed" to meeting it. The company has said that it is pressing ahead with tests of sustainable materials, including other recycled plastics and plastics made from alternative sources such as e-methanol.[48] At LEGO, as at the vast majority of companies that have begun the journey to a more sustainable future, the commitment remains undimmed. They are all too aware that their stakeholders of tomorrow will not accept the production methods of today.

That awareness was underlined again in October 2024 when three other prominent European companies—Gucci owner Kering, drugmaker GSK, and building materials producer Holcim—became the first to adopt science-based targets to protect nature established by the Science Based

Targets Network, a newly formed group that aims to reduce biodiversity loss resulting from human activity.[49] The three companies' commitments include conserving natural ecosystems, recycling water, and minimizing leakages.

Also in October 2024, ExxonMobil's chief executive, Darren Woods, told the annual UN Climate Change Conference in Azerbaijan that his company, the top oil and gas producer in the US, "will continue to advocate for the world to address greenhouse-gas emissions and the world needs to do this on a collective basis." Woods added that "I'm not sure how 'drill, baby, drill' [one of President Trump's oft-repeated mantras] translates into policy." He went even further in an interview with *The Economist*, cautioning Trump against scrapping the Biden administration's 2022 Inflation Reduction Act, which has offered subsidies and tax incentives for clean technologies in which ExxonMobil is now investing, and warning the president against leaving the Paris Agreement on climate change. "It doesn't benefit our country going in and out, in and out," Woods said.[50]

NO GOING BACK

As the above initiatives suggest, the future boardroom is less likely to be shaped by politicians or activists than by the realities of the world around us. Companies cannot afford to destabilize their financial and human capital by ignoring sustainability issues. They will have to satisfy the demands of critical outside stakeholders such as customers, suppliers, shareholders, and insurance providers. The company of the future will also have no choice but to respond to regulations requiring them to disclose the sustainability and climate competence of their directors and senior managers. These regulations will have the effect of creating an even playing field where key stakeholders can compare the performance of different companies.

The bottom line is that boards that are unable to make up their minds about their companies' purpose could find themselves saddled with more risk and less opportunity.

Whether we like it or not, Mother Nature keeps sending us invoices—and her collections department isn't messing around. Just turn on the news almost any day of the week. The litany of catastrophic events around the world caused by extreme weather—powerful hurricanes, devastating floods, scorching heat, wildfires, and more—never ends. The cost of pretending that these events are someone else's problem is mounting fast, and sure to become even greater as humanity struggles to find effective ways of halting and reversing the degradation of the planet. No wonder Miami-Dade County in Florida has appointed a chief heat officer to find ways of avoiding heat-related deaths and emergency department visits.[51]

Any board that does not pay attention to the consequences of these upheavals for its business is violating the trust of its stakeholders. The costs of such inaction will be ever more painful. Businesses that continue to pollute the environment without regard to the consequences can expect to be on the receiving end of lawsuits brought by aggrieved individuals, communities, activist groups, and even nature itself. Take the legislation passed by Panama in March 2023 which guarantees sea turtles the right to live and enjoy free passage along its coast. In welcoming the new law, the founder of a group that helped push for greater protection for the turtles told the Associated Press: "We will be able to hold governments, corporations and public citizens legally accountable for violations of the rights of sea turtles."[52]

Ecuador, Colombia, India, and Spain, among others, have begun to bestow legal privileges on bodies of water. Spain recognized the Mar Menor, one of Europe's largest and most endangered saltwater lagoons, as a legal person in the autumn of 2022. The lagoon, which is separated from the Mediterranean by a 20-kilometre (12-mile) sandbar, has been badly polluted by sewage, fertilizer, and waste from nearby mines. The new law, driven by grassroots activists, enshrines the lagoon's right "to exist as an ecosystem and to evolve naturally" and recognizes its right to protection, conservation, and restoration.[53]

Some countries are going even further, passing laws that make willful damage to the environment, or ecocide, a crime. As of late 2024, France, Ukraine, and Vietnam, among others, had adopted such laws, and many others are set to follow. Mexico's proposed bill provides for jail time of up to fifteen years and hefty fines. Katrín Jakobsdóttir, Iceland's prime minister from 2017 to early 2024, noted that while enforcing an ecocide law would be complicated, it is "only a matter of time before this issue becomes the biggest issue in the human rights arena."[54]

INSURANCE AS A DRIVER OF CHANGE

The risks from climate disasters are becoming especially onerous for the insurance industry. As natural disasters become more frequent and severe, insurers will be under mounting pressure to raise premiums, adjust coverage terms, or withdraw from high-risk markets altogether. This trend is already raising serious concerns for homeowners and businesses, particularly in regions most affected by climate change. Reinsurers, which provide financial protection to insurance companies by covering part of the risks they underwrite, are also confronting rising claims and consequently raising their rates.

Eric Andersen, president of Aon, one of the world's biggest insurance brokers, didn't mince his words in testimony to a US Senate committee in early 2023. Climate change, said Andersen, is destabilizing an industry built on risk prediction, creating "a crisis of confidence around the ability to predict loss," driving up prices and pushing insurers out of high-risk markets. "Just as the U.S. economy was overexposed to mortgage risk in 2008, the economy today is overexposed to climate risk," he added.[55]

Subsequent events bear out Andersen's warning. When Florida's state-run property insurer Citizens Property Insurance Corporation announced a 14 percent rate hike for 2025, it cited the financial strain from Hurricane Ian and rising reinsurance costs. The increase was part of an effort to stabilize its reserves and mitigate the risk of assessments on policyholders. Similarly, California's FAIR Plan for high-risk properties has grappled with surging enrollment as private insurers withdraw from wildfire-prone areas. Major carriers like State Farm and Allstate have stopped issuing new policies, driving more homeowners to the FAIR Plan, which has faced mounting deficits and growing calls for reform.

On the other side of the world, one of Australia's largest insurers, Suncorp, pushed up homeowner premiums by

9.9 percent in 2024 due in part to the sharp rise in claims from natural disasters, as well as inflation and the mounting cost of reinsurance. The Brisbane-based company said the hike would have been even bigger were it not for a cyclone protection pool for insurers backed by the federal government.[56] The pool acts as a risk-sharing mechanism, helping to stabilize premiums and ensuring that coverage remains available in cyclone-prone regions.

Despite the backlash against anything carrying an environmental, social, and governance label, pressures to toe the sustainability line are mounting faster than almost anyone expected just a few years ago. As Unilever's former chair Michael Treschow says, change is happening 24/7 without the luxury of time to digest—much less discuss—a response. That is another good reason for boards and senior executives to be prepared for more frequent and more intense scrutiny from their stakeholders, including insurance providers.

GREENWASHING BACKFIRES

Some companies have sought to evade accountability by turning to "greenwashing"—in other words, knowingly, or sometimes unknowingly, allowing themselves to convey a misleading impression of how products or services are environmentally sound, or pretending that they have a more positive impact on the environment than they actually do. Again, such tactics are unlikely to succeed for long in a world of growing transparency and activism. Thus, Deutsche Bank's investment arm was fined US$25 million by the US Securities and Exchange Commission in September 2023 for misstatements regarding its environmental, social, and governance (ESG) investment process.[57] The firm's former head of sustainability had alleged that it failed to live up to its promises to incorporate ESG factors into research and investment recommendations for ESG-related products. With the policing of greenwashing likely to tighten in many parts of the world, the board of the future would be wise to ensure that management comes clean on its progress towards sustainability.

STRATEGIES FOR THE FUTURE

In responding to sustainability skeptics, the board of the future will have to show enlightened leadership. The fact is that change has always been resisted. Think of the days when horses had to make way on the roads for cars and we had to build parking lots for cars, or when corruption was accepted as just another cost of business, or when the supply chain was only the supplier's problem, or when smoking was allowed on airplanes and considered glamorous.

Yet societies change and so—eventually—do our habits and choices. Change is never easy, especially for those who fear they will have less of what they want and like and are accustomed to.

This is where enlightened board leadership comes in. The director's fiduciary duty is to ensure that the company not only survives but thrives. That means accepting that today's status quo is not necessarily a better option than tomorrow's inevitably different and maybe even risky future.

I recommend the following steps as ways of discussing the transformation process and moving it along:

- Continue focusing on what you are good at while working to become more efficient and reducing your carbon, water, and negative externality footprint.

- Explore new business models that build on your proven expertise and equip you for resilience and a more sustainable future. In some companies the initial thrust may be on internal projects, while others will focus on acquiring or investing in outside businesses with the goal of opening new horizons and diversifying risk.

- Reinvent your company by, for example, transforming from a fossil fuel to a renewable energy producer or transitioning to a net-zero energy model.

- Position sustainability as a fundamental element of your company's strategy, reflecting a commitment that encompasses environmental stewardship, social responsibility, and ethical governance.

- Reimagine the way your products and services are delivered. For example, consider whether you should be selling your products or leasing them.

- Reimagine your products and business model and find partners to develop a "circular" business model that adds value without adding waste.

I use three criteria to judge whether boards are succeeding in these endeavours. First, are investors, banks, and customers willing to give their money to the company? Second, are employees willing to give their time and careers to the company? Third, are other stakeholders, such as suppliers and insurers, willing to place their trust in the company?

For an existing business, the transformation can be gradually phased in. A startup, on the other hand, has the advantage of being able to launch with a sustainable model fully in place. If and when it becomes an acquisition target, it can (hopefully) transfer its policies and culture to its new owners with a minimum of disruption.

More immediately, I have the following advice for boards:

Acknowledge and navigate complexity. The boardroom of tomorrow doesn't shy away from criticisms or conflicting perspectives. Instead, it actively engages to build trust, foster inclusivity, and uncover opportunities for innovation.

Communicate with precision and purpose. In a world flooded with information, clarity wins. Share your sustainability goals in a way that aligns seamlessly with your business strategy, free from jargon. Future-ready boards know how to craft messaging that connects with diverse audiences and inspires action.

Make sustainability a core business driver. Sustainability isn't a box to be checked. It's a competitive advantage. Show how integrating sustainability into operations future-proofs your company, sparks innovation, and creates shared value.

Balance performance and purpose. Financial success and sustainability are two sides of the same coin. The future boardroom should see them as mutually reinforcing, not conflicting, thereby weaving sustainability into the fabric of long-term strategy.

Activate a two-way dialogue with stakeholders. Whether hearing from employees or investors or the communities the company serves, the board of the future listens actively and engages meaningfully. Build partnerships that address stakeholder needs while driving forward-looking decisions.

Zero in on strategic priorities. With infinite demands on resources, the best boards focus on material issues—those with the greatest impact on the company and its stakeholders. A laser-sharp focus on what matters most will set the future boardroom apart.

Back decisions with data and vision. Boards of the future don't just talk—they show. Use robust data to highlight the tangible outcomes of sustainability initiatives, from cost savings to competitive differentiation. Let the numbers tell the story while keeping a bold vision in sight.

Stay adaptive and anticipatory. The pace of change is accelerating. Future boardrooms don't just react; they anticipate. Stay ahead of emerging standards, technologies, and practices, ensuring your strategy evolves with—and shapes—the business landscape.

The Conference Board has some useful advice on ways to build on these strategies.[58] The first step is to explain that environmental, social, and governance initiatives are a "natural extension" of a long-standing commitment to corporate responsibility. Instead of using the politically loaded term "ESG," many companies have come to favour "sustainability," which, as the Conference Board puts it, "may be better understood by employees, customers, and the public." Blackrock's

Larry Fink explained that he stopped using the term ESG not because he no longer believed in it but rather because the abbreviation had been "weaponized … (and) misused by the far left and the far right."[59] Indeed, he affirmed that Black-Rock would continue to engage with companies in which it invests on such crucial issues as decarbonization, corporate governance, and social justice.

There is no shortage of alternatives to the now-much-maligned abbreviations ESG and DEI. How about "sound judgment" or "business with integrity" or "competent governance" or "sustainable governance" or "quality governance" or "proactive governance"? The bottom line is that no matter what words we use, the principles behind environmental, social, and governance risks and opportunities are universal truths that every far-sighted board should embrace if it is serious about upholding its fiduciary duty.

The Conference Board also advises companies to proactively engage with politicians and others who have been at the forefront of the recent hostility towards ESG and DEI. I was honoured to address the annual Texas Energy Forum at the Petroleum Club of Houston in August 2023 and the Energy Transition Forum in Washington, DC, in December 2024, and invited back in February 2025. In each case, the audience would probably have paid little attention to my message in years gone by, but I could not have wished for a warmer or more attentive reception. While Houston remains the centre of the US oil and gas industry, it is also carving out a reputation as a hotbed for renewable energy innovation. And many policy-makers on both sides of the aisle in Washington remain committed to renewables as a critical component of the country's future energy security.

Directors and senior executives should lose no opportunity to explain why acting on environmental, social, and governance issues serves the interests not only of their business but also of politicians' constituents. Retreating from the broader public conversation about these issues risks forfeiting an opportunity to tell a company's story to stakeholders who may be taking an interest in sustainability issues for the first time. If your company fails to seize the initiative, other, less friendly players may step in, taking control of the conversation and raising the danger that you may end up having to correct mis- and disinformation. In getting their message across to the widest possible audience, companies should also consider joining forces to discuss the issues they are facing. Local, family-owned businesses can be especially effective allies as they are critical to their communities and generally well respected across the political spectrum.

Whatever the current frustrations with the sustainability movement, the pressing challenges that it represents for business deserve to be much more than three-letter political footballs. Environmental, social, and governance issues represent tangible, inescapable risks and opportunities that at one time or another will confront almost every business on the planet. Critics of sustainability, as well as present and future board members, would be wise to take note.

///

Ten Questions for the Board of the Future

1. How are you ensuring that sustainability drives profits, not just compliance, in your core business strategy?

2. Have you talked to your company's insurers and financial backers to see how they perceive the future of their business—and the impact on yours?

3. Is your board laser-focused on the sustainability issues that truly move the needle for your business?

4. How are you engaging with critics and skeptics to turn challenges into opportunities?

5. Can you confidently back up every sustainability claim you make with hard data and results?

6. Are you ready to tackle upcoming regulations that could expose gaps in your board's sustainability expertise?

7. What is your board doing to avoid being the next headline in greenwashing lawsuits?

8. Have you stress-tested your business against climate and nature risks that could drive up costs or disrupt operations?

9. Is your board bold enough to reinvent outdated business models before competitors beat you to it?

10. Is your board ready to lead decisively in a world where governance missteps aren't forgiven?

CHAPTER FOUR

Road Map to the Future

It is of the essence that board members are clear about their own personal purpose and values. Why are they on this board in the first place? What brings them there? How are they as boardroom members going to contribute to this organization making the world a better place? What are their personal values driving decision-making when complexity and stakes are high? The answers to these questions rest within ourselves and can be found through boardroom coaching.

—Annette Bak Kirby, top team effectiveness and boardroom coach, based in Abu Dhabi

Where do we start in designing the boardroom of the future? There is little doubt that an overhaul in the composition of corporate boards and how they function is both necessary and inevitable. The reasons are not hard to find.

The board of the future will have many more responsibilities than its predecessors and be accountable to many more stakeholders. Its work will be more complex, going well beyond the traditional tasks of reviewing financial statements and overseeing management's performance. It will pay closer attention to sustainability and stakeholder relationships. The board of the future will also take a longer view, less concerned about the next quarter or even the next year than about the forces that will affect the business for decades to come. It will put more work into trying to foresee the geopolitical,

73

macroeconomic, and natural forces likely to shape the company's future, and how to respond to them.

In taking on these extra burdens, the board will have access to far more information and sophisticated technology than its predecessors. What it will not have more of, however, is perhaps the scarcest resource of all: time. Board members tend to be busy people and no one enjoys meetings that drag on or run late. Getting organized, whether that means having the right mix of committees or ensuring that board members are not burdened with unnecessary reading material, will thus be a key ingredient of the future board's success. Kathleen Taylor, chair of Element Fleet Management and former Royal Bank of Canada chair, explains:

> Making sure the board is effective is a hard thing to do when there's so much information in front of us. That means being very mindful about setting agendas and timetables, making sure management is helping to focus the board on the most important topics for the board's attention, not cluttering up the time together with reports on how hard everybody has been working on different initiatives. It is all about driving for impact in meetings by getting the board's best advice on the most difficult issues facing management at that point in time.
>
> I would say that the most important thing board chairs and committee chairs can do to help the board function effectively, in the face of monstrous amounts of new information, new challenges, and dilemmas posing hurdles to the business, is to work really closely with management on advance planning for the board sessions. There's the old expression that great outcomes are 10 percent strategy and

90 percent execution. But if you dig deeper, great execution in my opinion is 10 percent doing and 90 percent planning.

HOW BIG SHOULD THE FUTURE BOARD BE?

In spite of their mounting workload, boards have generally shrunk over the years and experts agree that is probably a good thing. The larger a board becomes, the greater the risk of inefficiency and tensions in the decision-making process. Worst of all, experience has shown that the quality of individual directors tends to decline as the board expands. "Empirical studies … have mostly found negative correlations between board size and firm performance," concluded the authors of an April 2023 paper for the *Harvard Law School Forum on Corporate Governance*.[60] Using the example of German boards, which are typically much larger than those in other countries due to their two-tier structure, they observed that "we find robust evidence that forcing firms to have large boards is detrimental."

Small and agile should be the motto of the board of the future. As Kathleen Taylor puts it:

> You need to be big enough to get all the work done, but small enough for conversations to be very pointed, focused, and courageous. Members need to have room and time to express their concerns, ask their questions, and really get into the meat of what it is that management is trying to engage the board on.

From my interviews with business leaders, the consensus seems to be that a board of eight to ten members and no more than twelve tends to work best. Bear in mind, however, that the chair is the conductor, and some conductors are more comfortable with a bigger (or smaller) number of players than others.

MORE COMMITTEES, FEWER COMMITTEES, OR NEWER COMMITTEES?

"Boards need to operate more like teams," says Dominic Barton, chair of Rio Tinto and McKinsey's former global managing director. One of the best ways of accomplishing that is through the judicious use of committees and, occasionally, working groups. Well-chosen, smoothly functioning committees can contribute significantly to board and corporate performance. But pick the wrong ones and a board can soon find itself chasing the wrong priorities, spinning its wheels, or bogged down in turf battles.

The first step is to examine the board's purpose and determine which committees best fit that purpose. The Competent Boards global future boardroom survey asked respondents to name three committees that are not commonly seen on today's boards but are likely to be needed in the years to come. We received a wide variety of responses, underlining the need both for fresh thinking and for each board to tailor its choices to its own priorities. Below are the committees most often suggested by respondents in order of number of mentions, together with a brief description of each one's purpose:

- **Sustainability committee.** Focusing on environmental, social, and governance issues, working to integrate sustainability into the company's strategy, transforming to a circular economy.

- **Digital transformation and technology committee.** Overseeing digital strategy, including matters related to cybersecurity, artificial intelligence, data management, and technological innovations.

- **Risk and compliance committee.** An expanded risk committee monitoring all forms of risk, including environmental, social, governance, digital, and regulatory risks, to ensure the company's resilience.

- **Human capital committee.** Focusing on human resources, preparing the company for future workforce trends and challenges, and looking for ways to attract, retain, and develop relevant skills. This committee will also provide oversight in relation to justice, equity, and inclusion with a view to fostering a diverse and inclusive culture suited to the company and its strategy.

- **Future opportunities committee.** Evaluating and reporting on future trends and potential opportunities for the business.

- **Strategic partnerships committee.** Overseeing and cultivating strategic partnerships and collaborations that benefit the business.

- **AI ethics and data governance committee.** Managing ethical issues related to data use and digital technologies, including artificial intelligence, to ensure responsible and ethical use of data.

- **Ethics, trust, and transparency committee.** Overseeing ethical conduct, fostering trust in and outside the company, and maintaining transparency in all operations and decision-making.

- **Stakeholder engagement committee.** Managing relations with a wide range of stakeholders, ensuring effective communication and engagement on relevant issues.

- **Organizational design and self-management advisory committee.** Offering advice on structural changes within the organization, including models like self-management to increase agility and responsiveness.

- **A separate nature committee.** Focusing specifically on the company's impact on nature, the environment, conservation efforts, regenerative efforts, and compliance with expected nature and environmental regulations.

Several respondents, it should be said, were opposed to adding any new committees at all, or favoured consolidating existing ones to avoid diluting focus or adding complexity to the board's work. In considering new committees or broadening the scope of existing ones, former Unilever chairman Michael Treschow sounds another important note of caution: "Don't undermine management by having all sorts of committees doing what is really management's job." As Treschow sees it, a new committee should be reserved for a complicated and difficult issue that requires a lot of attention from the board, rather than being set up just because an issue is important. Likewise, Dominic Barton suggests that technology issues may sometimes best be handled by an advisory committee comprising a broad set of experts. Such a group may report to a management team member, and board members are free to join its conversations if they wish.

AGILITY IS KEY

The Competent Boards global network also has some valuable advice on how board committees should function in the future. Former Royal Dutch Shell and Bank of America chairman Chad Holliday says that a board should typically set up a special committee for only a limited time to delve into a specific issue and come up with appropriate recommendations. Citing the specific case of cybersecurity, Holliday notes that regular briefings by outside specialists can often be more productive than setting up a committee or appointing a board member with specialist expertise in a particular area. As far as normal committee work goes, far too much time is spent on compensation issues, Holliday believes.

The board of the future should focus on developing small, well-run committees that meet the needs of the times, says Joyce Cacho, chair of Sistema Biobolsa and a director of several other companies:

> I foresee a time when regulators will catch up with this kind of agile structure. For listed companies, it might not be too far-fetched to predict a future where the traditional three standing committees might be deemed insufficient for effective oversight by regulators.
>
> Some boards already have standing sustainability or ESG committees. For these companies, transitioning to any new standing committee structure might be relatively easy.

But for others that continue to do the bare minimum of stopping at current US SEC compliance, changes to the standing committee structure could be on the horizon. These organizations need to realize that simply adhering to the minimum requirements may not ensure their survival and success in the evolving corporate landscape.

THE ROLE OF INCENTIVES

The board has a key role—arguably even *the* key role—in driving the changes that will turn the boardroom of the future into the company of the future. Achieving such a transition requires much more than memos and training sessions, especially in the upper echelons of management. Few tools are more effective than tying at least a portion of executive pay to sustainability performance.

As Andrew Behar at As You Sow notes:

CEOs can get stuff done if they're incentivized properly. And that's the responsibility of the board. It's how the board controls strategy execution. If you want a company to still be in business ten or twenty years from now, you have got to incentivize the CEO to shift the company's strategy to reduce risk and adapt to a changing landscape in terms of supply chains, negative impact on your community, and building an inclusive and attractive culture for employees and customers.

The question is: What form should those incentives take, and what should they reward? All too often up to now, a higher share price has been the main yardstick used to measure the performance of board members and senior managers. While the share price is indisputably one measurement of a company's success, it is likely to play a smaller role than before in the boardroom (and the management suite) of the future. "What we can try and do as board members is to ensure that we are allocating resources in a smart way that serves all of our stakeholders, that we're not overpromising, and we're realizing that we're entrusted with the value of the company over the medium and longer term, and not just today's stock price," says Eric Wetlaufer, a director of Canada's TMX Group and the Investment Management Corporation of Ontario. He adds for emphasis that "anybody who keeps looking at today's stock price should be barred from working at the company. There's nothing wrong with a short-term view of projects and accomplishments, but the rewards should be greatest for longer-term accomplishments."

A study of more than one thousand companies by consultancy WTW, where Competent Boards network member Shai Ganu is the global leader of executive compensation and board advisory services, found that no fewer than 81 percent used some form of environmental, social, and governance performance measurement in 2024 to determine executive incentives, up from 75 percent the previous year.[61] The proportion ranges from 76 percent in the US to 93 percent in Europe. Even in the US and Canada, measurement of sustainability in long-term incentive plans has grown significantly—but still lags behind Europe. The components include environmental and climate, people and human resources, diversity and inclusion, health and safety, customer, and governance measures. It's worth noting that

US companies tend to use qualitative indicators to evaluate sustainability performance, while three-quarters of European companies measure it quantitatively. As WTW notes, "The incorporation of ESG metrics in executive incentive plans has become prevalent practice, while each industry emphasizes ESG factors with the greatest impact to the long-term value creation of their businesses."[62]

New York University's Tensie Whelan estimates that companies which already tie executive pay to sustainability performance typically give sustainability a weight of about 20 percent in determining bonuses and other incentive payments. However, she notes, because boards tend not to be involved in sustainability strategy, the targets set to measure performance may not be the most relevant or the most useful.

When it comes to measuring sustainability performance, Frederic Barge, founder of Reward Value, a non-profit executive pay consultancy based in the Netherlands, advises companies to stick to those variables most relevant to their operations. He points to the Dutch health and nutrition group DSM, which splits its long-term incentive program roughly equally between financial and non-financial performance, with just two non-financial yardsticks: energy efficiency and emissions. Since the group's merger with Swiss-based Firmenich in 2023, the energy efficiency target has been replaced by a social target on diversity and inclusion.

Barge adds that employers should draw a distinction between short- and long-term incentives. The Swedish telecoms group Ericsson used only long-term incentives for a while to reward its top leaders beyond their base salary (although it reintroduced a short-term incentive in 2023). Short-term incentives tend to have more impact at lower levels of management, where operational performance is more relevant than setting strategic goals or spurring innovation.

Barge urges the future board to focus on the following:

- **The appropriate criteria.** "In some instances," he cautions, "companies tend to go with the flow and use what is popular at the time and just put a lot of different elements into a bucket of sustainability or ESG." Instead, he recommends choosing those most relevant to the company's purpose and strategy. However, one element that no company can afford to ignore is inequality, Barge says. "The credibility of organizations will be negatively impacted if we have excessive remuneration. I think that next to climate and geopolitical forces, inequality is really influencing our future significantly."

- **The company's reputation.** Barge explains: "If I can't really measure specific impacts or it becomes difficult to incorporate them into my remuneration policy, what I can do is measure my reputation against four key stakeholders: employees, customers, supply chain, and society at large. Nowadays, most of the value that we measure is no longer on the balance sheet, it's really intangible assets. Reputation is a key element of that. So having it involved in your remuneration program is a logical direction to take. And it's something that can be monitored and measured with external parties, and therefore gives more credibility than having more difficult-to-define social targets."

- **The most appropriate time horizon.** For chief executives, some incentives may only kick in after they have left the company, when the board and stakeholders have an opportunity to judge the full extent of their legacy. The Swiss pharmaceuticals group Roche (Hoffmann-La Roche) stretches deferred share options for its chief executive over a period as long as ten years.

- **The right components.** "Once you start to carve (an incentive plan) up into little pieces, it will lose its power in really steering behaviour," Barge notes. "Because if each counts for maybe 1 or 2 percent, it's not going to move the needle and make you behave differently. If it counts for 20 percent of your incentive, then it becomes more important, and you start to behave around it. The current practice is for companies to focus much more on financial key performance indicators than non-financial ones. The average weighting of a single non-financial indicator is less than a quarter of the average financial one. But such a wide difference gives the wrong signal to executives about the appropriate attention they should give to non-financial performance indicators. It also signals to the outside world that non-financial performance is of lesser importance than financial results. It is time for companies to apply equal focus to financial and non-financial performance."

Francesca Ecsery, who serves on five boards and has chaired several remuneration committees, favours an incremental but broad-based approach to sustainability incentives:

Frankly, something is better than nothing. Money talks. My attitude is, little steps. Also, that it's not just at the top, but galvanizes the whole company. The financial key performance indicators are probably 70–80 percent of the bonus structure, but then you've got another 20–30 percent that you can flag for some personal objectives or strategic ESG project. You can mix and match depending on the individual and how much influence they have on each of these.

Ecsery also points to the importance of having a chief executive who understands the power of remuneration and is able to use it as a lever to galvanize the troops. As a board member, she takes an interest in the incentives provided to management one layer below the chief executive and chief financial officer. "We don't want to interfere, but we do want to make sure that whatever we give you is being cascaded down. If the incentives just stay at the top, who is going to help you deliver those objectives?"

SOME OTHER CHANGES ON THE HORIZON

Many other changes are on the way in the boardroom of the future. Among others, we can expect an erosion of the long-standing belief among some directors—at least in public companies and especially in the US—that their primary duty is to represent the interests of specific shareholders. While owners, in other words equity holders, will continue to vote for the directors of a company, board members will come under mounting pressure to consider the impact of their decisions on *all* the company's stakeholders in both the short and long term rather than just one particular investor.

I discuss the importance of comprehensive stakeholder engagement in chapter eight. Suffice to say for now that governance codes around the world increasingly underscore this shift towards a "stakeholder-inclusive approach." Here's what the Institute of Directors of South Africa's *Guidance for Boards* has to say on the subject:

> The rationale for a major shareholder and/or other stake-holder appointing a director to the board should be that they have appointed a trusted person who they believe has the necessary experience and competence, and who will behave in the above manner. The objective should not be to appoint a director who will champion the cause of action beneficial to that shareholder or stakeholder. Notwithstanding a shareholder or stakeholder's legal right to appoint certain directors, the role of the nominations committee or another such committee performing such role is still crucial to determine and give recommendations on the requirements of the board and most appropriate fit for a director.
>
> Adopting a stakeholder inclusive approach means the board as part of its broader stakeholder engagement may, under certain circumstances, seek input from stakeholders to identify what stakeholders believe may be an appropriate course of action. One of these stakeholders may be a major shareholder, constituency or creditor who has appointed a director to the board. In this instance the director may serve as a conduit for relaying the views of the shareholder or stakeholder. However, the director must still act (including

when making decisions) in the best interests of the company on whose board he or she serves.[63]

Even the prosaic briefing materials that board members receive are due for an overhaul. Kathleen Taylor notes that just as a board cannot do its job properly without the right skill sets around the table, it also needs to be properly briefed:

> Board materials need to be board-ready materials and can't be repurposed management materials. They need to be at a level that directors can digest and understand without an unnecessary "Easter egg hunt" to get themselves deeply into the problems that management is trying to solve.
>
> Time together is every board's scarcest resource, so we need to step back and ask ourselves: Are our materials facilitating the best use of our time at the meeting? Or are the materials so voluminous that we have no idea what the main issue is that needs to be discussed? Or are they materials that everybody took the time to read but then they are not in focus?

Pulling it all together, the *Code of Conduct for Directors* published in October 2024 by the United Kingdom's Institute of Directors spells out six principles that, I believe, offer a universal yardstick for measuring a board's performance:

- **Leading by example.** Demonstrating exemplary standards of behaviour in personal conduct and decision-making.

- **Integrity.** Acting with honesty, adhering to strong ethical values, and doing the right thing.

- **Transparency.** Communicating, acting and making decisions openly, honestly and clearly.

- **Accountability.** Taking personal responsibility for actions and their consequences.

- **Fairness.** Treating people equitably, without discrimination or bias.

- **Responsible business.** Integrating ethical and sustainable practices into business decisions, taking into account societal and environmental impacts.[64]

GREEN WISHING VERSUS GREEN PERFORMANCE

One of the toughest challenges for the board of the future will be to move from good intentions to good (and, even better, excellent) performance. That includes giving sustainability the time and attention it deserves. Daouii Abouchere, director of sustainable investing for Europe, the Middle East, and Africa at Wellington Management, warns of the dangers of being either too timid or too ambitious:

> Sustainability is nuanced. Whether it's the climate crisis or the need for effective labour management, understanding what others are doing and understanding best practices is important. But being able to understand what we should prioritize and how we should integrate these best practices to help us on our journey is even more important. Not every aspect is relevant to every company, and that is perfectly okay. But it's also perfectly okay to showcase that we

are on a multi-year journey towards getting us to be a lot more robust, sustainability driven, and forward looking.

THE IMPORTANCE OF A SKILLS MATRIX

The journey cannot start without first putting a board skills matrix in place and finding the best possible candidates to fill the various roles needed to oversee the future direction of the company. These tasks should be a higher priority than determining the size of the board or committee mandates. Kathleen Taylor describes some of the tricky decisions involved:

> Boards will always be threading the needle between the competencies they need around the table and the number of members they would like to have. It really does put at a premium the ability to attract directors who come with multiple sets of skills. We're always going to need a chair of an audit committee who understands the ins and outs of building and reading and utilizing financial statements and other disclosure materials. But it's great if that person has also run an organization, has had lots of people reporting to them, and has had geographic spread if the company is an international one, to name a few examples.
>
> Boards need to do a great job of thinking about longer-term succession at the board table, reflecting on the needs of the business, the gaps that might be created by the retirement of existing board members, or the gaps being created by changes in the business and the environment, always keeping a live set of "straw models" of "ideal" directors to keep track of much-needed competencies going forward.

Of course, it's rare that you match those precise competencies with a specific human being, but you do a lot better than if you didn't have the lists of great-to-have, nice-to-have, and oh-my-god-wouldn't-it-be-fantastic if the person also brought this with them. You then try to find those traits across as many new recruits given the size and shape of your board.

The process that Taylor describes can be a bit of a chicken-and-egg situation. On one hand, every board aspires to having the most competent people deliberating on the issues most material to the business. On the other, an assessment of those issues may be needed before decisions can be taken on what skills are needed around the table. My prediction is that this conundrum will be solved by much greater use of outside advisers to examine relevant trends and issues.

KEEP SUSTAINABILITY FRONT AND CENTRE

However it's done, the board can then turn its attention to identifying the issues most material to the business, in terms of not only financial performance, as has been the case in the past, but also long-term sustainability. Once that exercise is complete, it can start setting targets. Daouii Abouchere advises avoiding flashy goals far in the future that can be derailed by any number of unexpected developments over which the company has no control. Instead, she says, "the real power is showcasing how you are fundamentally transforming year by year and incorporating what's materially relevant to you into your overall strategy."

Many boards fall into the trap of doing little more than reviewing management reports instead of encouraging tangible initiatives to improve sustainability. As Tensie Whelan notes, the board of the future would be well advised to take a more strategic and proactive approach to matters such as key performance indicators, linking compensation to sustainability targets, and capital allocation for projects that enhance sustainability. It will have to ask more probing questions to identify the full range of material risks and opportunities related to sustainability. And then it will have to set performance indicators that encourage innovation rather than just comprehensive reporting.

When it comes to allocating capital resources, sustainability all too often drops to the bottom of the priority list because management sees it only as an expense rather than as a way to drive improved financial performance. The board needs to get far more involved, Whelan says, "to ensure that on material issues, there is the capital investment needed to position the company for a challenging future, as opposed to just saying 'it's like a risk or an opportunity somewhere in the future that we don't really understand so we can't justify making this investment in the face of a weak economy,' or whatever."

Yoshiko Shibasaka, a Japanese member of the IFRS Foundation's Integrated Reporting and Connectivity Council, adds that sustainability is a "very critical" management issue and that management therefore needs to be involved in its many facets. However, she notes that the degree of involvement in specific areas can vary widely by country, by industry, and by individual company. "Companies should do a materiality analysis based on their own business model, their strong points, their purpose, their vision and mission," Shibasaka advises. Sustainability risks would obviously be an important element of this exercise, again taking into account a company's particular circumstances. Once these issues have been clarified, decisions on a suitable investment policy becomes much easier.

One reason companies have not given sustainability the attention it deserves may be that too few boards appreciate the full impact of decarbonization on the bottom line or the scarcity of natural resources—think water—that are all too often taken as a given. Transparency on climate and other sustainability risks can help reassure investors and open doors to new sources of capital. Based on recent research at NYU, Whelan gives some examples of sectors and companies that have come to realize the benefits of sustainability:

> If you look at the automotive sector, there are three areas that really drive financial performance improvements related to sustainability. One is around waste management. We worked with one company that, through things like reusing solvent or putting components of old cars into new cars, was generating about US$235 million of benefit on an annual basis, which they did not know. They did not know because their accounting systems—and this is for all companies—did not track avoided cost. A big part of the benefits of sustainability are around avoiding costs—energy costs, water costs, pollution costs, reputational risk costs, volatility costs, all of those things. If you don't include them, then you don't recognize the submerged part of the iceberg in terms of how much benefit you have.

Working with Eileen Fisher, an apparel company, we saw that they had shifted away from air freight towards shipping and trucking, which saved them about US$1.5 million a year. They also invested in the circularity of their clothing and created a new project called Renew, where they were able, for no money, to engage younger consumers whom they hadn't been able to reach before. There was no marketing campaign. You bring in your old clothes for a coupon, and they resell them for you. We worked with REI Co-op, another apparel and activewear company known for its focus on sustainability and purpose. That focus improved their employee retention and productivity so much. No company tracks the benefit of those programs, and yet they are integral to the business. So there are all kinds of ways in which companies are benefiting financially.

Using another example, Mahindra's former chief sustainability officer Anirban Ghosh issues an even more forceful call to action:

I understand the need to balance profits for today with the needs of the future. But unless we are proactive about it, the process is going to be very slow. I'm hearing these days that clothes made from banana plant fibre are great to wear and great for the environment. But some textile company has to proactively start that movement. Initially, the clothes will be expensive, but we'll have to make them mainstream.

///

Ten Questions for the Board of the Future

1. As the director of a company, whose interests do you think you represent?

2. How much planning goes into your board meetings? Name three ways in which this process can be improved.

3. Name three ways for your board to function more efficiently. Have you shared these thoughts with other board members? If not, why not?

4. How many members does your board have? Could that number be reduced?

5. Would your board benefit from setting up any new committees? If so, what would they be?

6. Could any of your board committees be combined or eliminated?

7. Can you name one area where your board has seized the initiative in making the transition to a more sustainable future?

8. How often are sustainability issues on the agenda of your board meetings? How much time is devoted to these issues at each meeting and during a full year?

9. Are sustainability issues an integral part of all discussions on strategy and budget allocation?

10. Do you have trouble plowing through your board materials? If so, what can be done to lighten the load?

CHAPTER FIVE

Competence, Curiosity, Courage, Compassion...

The work to become a great director is a never-ending journey that we all need to take very seriously. It is all part of our personal growth and development.

—Kathleen Taylor, former chair, Royal Bank of Canada, and former chief executive, Four Seasons Hotels and Resorts

The concept of what makes the ideal corporate board has gone through several iterations over the past few decades. At one time companies vied to attract the biggest names in politics, business, and academia to their boards, whether a former US secretary of state, a former army chief of staff, or the retired head of a respected university. Relevant nuts-and-bolts experience seemed a secondary consideration. A sea change followed the publication in 1992 of the UK's seminal Cadbury report on corporate governance.[65] Board recruiters quickly turned their attention to experts in various areas of a company's business. Every board needed at least one financial specialist, a smart corporate lawyer, and perhaps an engineer, a marketing guru, or a banker, depending on its business. More recently, the emphasis shifted to what retired Tata Sons executive director R. Gopalakrishnan calls the competitive board, where, in his words, "each director is trying to prove that he's a bit more valuable than the person sitting next to him."

Now, the recognition is unfolding that the director of the future is likely to be a much different creature from the typical board member of today. The differences will be vast and numerous, running the gamut from age and ethnic origin to candidates with less interest in next week's share price and more in the varied constituencies and issues that shape the company's business. As Kristjan Jespersen, associate professor at the Copenhagen Business School, puts it: "What we will need to think about in the future is whether the composition of the board is able to meet the critical material risks that the company faces."

The extent of the coming transformation is clear from the Competent Boards future boardroom survey. When asked to name skills or traits that are commonly held by current directors but will be less relevant in the future, respondents' top pick was "traditional financial acumen." This confirms one of the central tenets of this book—namely, that no board can afford to focus on the financial statements and the share price without considering the non-financial forces that influence a company's business and, by extension, its overall stability. The realization is growing that companies will have to integrate their financial strategy into broader business and societal goals to a much greater extent than they have in the past.

This chapter spells out some of these competencies in greater detail, as well as ways in which boards can be encouraged to acquire them.

LOOK AROUND CORNERS AND SEIZE THE INITIATIVE

The number-one attribute of a competent board in the future will be initiative—in other words, an eagerness to tackle proactively the many daunting challenges that business is set to face. When it comes to compliance, for example, the board will be well advised to get a head start on new laws and regulations by implementing rigorous systems to capture data and report the results even before such disclosure becomes mandatory. Directors who are aware of voluntary standards and reporting trends can ask questions that will make their company an early adopter and thus able to shape what its peers and competitors are expected to report.

Every board will need to choose whether it wants to be a follower, waiting for customers and other stakeholders to prod it into action, or whether it makes more sense to be a leader and talk to investors, customers, employees, and others about the need to share certain information on the business. Discussing what is material to the business can help shape strategy by identifying looming opportunities and risks. Furthermore, those ahead of the pack can give regulators and lawmakers valuable information, helping the latter adjust policies and priorities to ensure a level playing field while, at the same time, gaining the competitive advantage that comes from being proactive.

A board cannot necessarily assume that management is complying with relevant regulations and standards, much less peering beyond the horizon to see what the future has in store. In an ever more complex world where rules often differ from one country to another (and even between states and between provinces), the board should consider investing in a solid enterprise risk management system and compliance trackers. Internal and external auditors should also be involved, not just in checking past performance indicators but also helping to identify future threats and opportunities. A competent board with access to up-to-date technology can go a long way towards ensuring that these systems are in place.

Seizing the initiative means having a mindset that is eager to look into the future and ready to expect the unexpected. In other words, the board of the future will want to peer around corners even if it isn't always clear what surprises are lurking there. The way to do this is to encourage input from the widest possible range of voices, engage those people in candid conversations, and then try to make sense of the information gathered. The board needs to weigh short- and long-term considerations. It must use technology almost in real time to analyze the information at its disposal.

Directors can learn a thing or two from airline pilots who decidedly change course to take account of shifting weather patterns or nearby aircraft. Pilots rely on a host of support systems both in and outside the plane, including air traffic controllers along their route, pilots of other planes around them, and, not least, their co-pilots. They are trained to make quick decisions when the unexpected happens. Likewise, directors who seek out the best advice and work as a team, respecting each other, senior management, and stakeholders, will surely be best equipped to guide their companies on smooth flights to safe landings.

WHO WILL BE THE DIRECTORS OF THE FUTURE?

C IS FOR COMPETENCE ... AND MANY OTHER QUALITIES

For me, ten attributes, all starting with the letter C, capture the most valuable hallmarks of future board directors. They are (in no specific order):

1. Competence
2. Curiosity
3. Courage
4. Compassion
5. Conscience
6. Confidence
7. Collaboration
8. Continuing education
9. Communication
10. Critical thinking

Board recruiters have often tended to look for candidates who can plug a specific gap around the boardroom table—say, an engineer, or a woman, or perhaps someone with knowledge of the Middle East because that's where the company has a large presence or is planning to expand. And companies understandably still take great pride in announcing that a new director is a well-respected former chief executive, or a recently retired government official, or the founder of some whiz-bang Silicon Valley startup.

However, boards are now moving in a different direction. Joyce Cacho, an independent director and chair of Sistema Biobolsa, says she pays no attention to announcements that dwell on a new director's formal titles:

> They are shorthand for a set of skills that people putting together position descriptions for board roles have not taken the time to unpack. Role descriptions embed historical biases. If you look at the marketplace, the number of women who can authentically claim the moniker of former CEO, sitting CEO, former CFO, sitting CMO are few and far between. And so you're fostering a smaller marketplace for filling that board seat and you're encouraging groupthink, both of which we know are not part of a winning boardroom.

> The characteristics that I would look forward to seeing around the board table are characteristics of leadership, not necessarily in the workplace. Many who come from systematically under-represented communities are typically overlooked for C-suite roles, where ability to put vision into action and lead people is traditionally demonstrated.

> They solve that systemic issue by demonstrating these skills elsewhere. They do it on the weekend, in social organizations, in their communities.

> We want leadership for sure, and we want leadership that understands accountability. I think we need to couch it in those very plain and transparent terms, rather than "sitting CEO," "former CEO or CFO," or other "former" traditional C-suite roles.

Cacho's views are borne out by Competent Boards future boardroom survey, which asked respondents to identify what they saw as the single most important category of skills for future board members. Almost two-thirds plumped for "soft" skills—emotional intelligence, adaptability, and strategic thinking, to name a few—rather than expertise in any specific field.

These issues are among the topics that PwC expects to shape board agendas in 2025.[66] As its report notes:

> Board composition, in terms of both individual and collective quality and decision-making ability, directly influences board performance and long-term shareholder value. A board that proactively assesses its skill sets, addresses director tenure, incorporates outcomes from board assessments and plans for succession can help guide the company toward future success. Directors have the power to make real change happen—and enhance effectiveness when it's needed most.

SKILLS YOU WILL NEED

Members of the Competent Boards network have a broad range of ideas, some of them overlapping, of the skills likely to be in greatest demand in the future boardroom. Kathleen Taylor has an especially succinct list that she learned from Stephen Jarislowsky, founder of the Canadian Coalition for Good Governance: "When I think about the necessary traits for directors, I think about what I call the three Cs: competency, curiosity, and courage," she says.

South African corporate governance guru Mervyn King puts a high value on intellectual honesty. "You've got to leave behind past experiences, your own needs, your own biases, and that takes intellectual effort," King notes. "Think of success in a sustainable manner, not just making profit at any cost. Success means adding value to society. You've got to cross what I call the Rubicon of intellectual honesty. It's integrity and fairness. You can only act fairly if you know and understand the needs, interests, and expectations of your stakeholders."

Wisdom, common sense, and sound judgment are at the top of R. Gopalakrishnan's list. "In all-important matters of human progress, technical knowledge itself will not work if you need behavioural knowledge—the ability to apply it and carry people with you," he says. "And in the world of corporate governance, it's that aspect that has to be reinforced."

Shailesh Haribhakti, another prominent Indian director and sustainability proponent, singles out integrity, honesty, and an ability to listen and respect diverse opinions as critical qualities for board members. "I would be looking for people who have a heart of gold," he says. "If you are not delivering value to the people who are sitting around the board table, then you are not fulfilling the remit that you are supposed to fulfill."

As the importance of these "soft" attributes grows, fewer seats on the board are likely to be reserved for specialists and more for generalists with a wider view of the world around them.

Eric Wetlaufer, former head of the CPP Investment Board's public markets investment department, elaborates:

> Take a look at what happens, starting in business schools. It used to be that you had marketing classes, finance classes,

organizational behaviour classes, and you specialized in one area. You'd build a career in that field, climbing straight up the ladder. Many board members of the past—and to some extent, even today—follow that mould. They bring deep expertise in one area of business to the board, and ideally, the skills matrix around the table checks all the necessary boxes. Directors review reports, prepare diligently, and contribute their specific expertise in board meetings.

But the future calls for board members with a broader range of experiences—people who have worked across industries, geographies, and capabilities. Younger professionals are already charting these diverse paths. They're zigging and zagging in their careers, experimenting with different roles, industries, and organizations. They're taking on hybrid positions—chief experience officer, chief innovation officer, and other inventive titles. These are the people in their thirties, not their sixties, who bring fresh perspectives. They're out there—we just need to find them.

Unfortunately, many search firms aren't doing a great job of uncovering these kinds of candidates. This has been a persistent frustration for me, especially with larger firms that tend to recycle the same "usual suspects" whom you could have called yourself. Smaller boutique firms, on the other hand, have shown more creativity in sourcing diverse and dynamic talent. There are individuals who've moved extensively around the corporate world, bringing a wealth of insights. The talent exists; we just need to raise our expectations and demand more from our search efforts.

The emergence of this new type of director doesn't mean that every member of the board should be a generalist with little or no experience of the company's particular sector. "A board that doesn't understand the industry could take a company in a very bad direction," notes Chad Holliday, a former chairman of Royal Dutch Shell and Bank of America. Holliday recalls that during the 2008–9 financial crisis, the US Federal Reserve directed that all but two members of the Bank of America board (of whom he was one) should have a deep financial background in the banking business:

> That's not the right way to go either. They all think they're experts because they were in the business. You can't get enough time for other topics. I think there has to be a balance. I would like to see at least two people on the board who have some experience of the industry. And I would like to know the character and quality of those people because, if I felt they were going to dominate the board, that would be a problem.

Some Competent Boards members cite an important exception to the trend away from specialists. Noting that health-care providers have increasingly brought academics, especially experts in specific diseases, onto their boards, Tensie Whelan, director of New York University's Stern Center for Sustainable Business, takes the view that experts in sustainability could be an especially valuable resource for a board. Examples of suitable candidates might include a respected chief sustainability officer, someone who has run a renewable energy company, an environmental, social, and governance–oriented investor who has made a real impact, or a senior executive at a major non-profit involved in climate science.

Even as recruiters and nominating committees review the criteria for board membership, aspiring directors should do some serious soul-searching of their own about their suitability for a board appointment. The days are fast coming to an end when a senior executive could retire in the expectation that he or she would be inundated with board offers on the basis of a long and distinguished career. As Jane Diplock, supervisory board member of the World Benchmarking Alliance and a former director of the Singapore Exchange, puts it: "Anyone who sees a board appointment as somehow a retirement job rather than an active job is not the person you want on your board."

LEARN, LEARN, LEARN

The members of John Deere's board had a problem a few years ago. They were so busy that they had little time to absorb the piles of briefing materials that they received on the storied farm-equipment maker's business. So they decided to draw up a list of specific topics that they felt they needed to be more familiar with. The company then set about compiling informative materials that would expand the directors' knowledge in those fields. One example was a forty-minute video on the ABCs of export controls put together with the help of the company's trade specialists and lawyers. "My guess is there's probably about thirty topics like that in a board," says Chad Holliday, one of Deere's directors at the time.

Deere's initiative highlights the importance of continuing education for corporate directors. Yes, experience is valuable, but in the fast-moving world of today, directors cannot afford to rest on their laurels and pretend that the knowledge they acquired in the past is adequate for the present or future.

That is especially true in a world where previously unfamiliar topics—think climate change, biodiversity, and artificial intelligence, to name three—have emerged as critical risks to almost every business. "Now we need to climb the ladder very rapidly and understand concepts that we've never really understood before," says Carolynn Chalmers, chief executive of the Good Governance Academy, based in South Africa. At the most basic level, Chalmers points to the maze of abbreviations—ISSB, IFRS, SSPs, ESRS, CSRD, TCFD, and so on—that can trip up those who have not yet taken the time to learn the ins and outs of climate change.

"There is a whole new language that we need to explore and discover," says Chalmers. "It means that everybody needs to have some background and needs to learn how to speak this new language. And not only just speak the new language, but actually understand what it means and experience what it means so that we can make informed decisions."

Board education can take many forms, from Deere's video on export controls to a two-day offsite briefing on cybersecurity to enrolling at an organization, such as Competent Boards, specifically geared to the needs of board members. "I don't think there's one road to heaven," says Jane Diplock. "There are lots and lots of ways in which boards and individuals can educate themselves."

We should not ignore what directors can learn from each other by serving on a board. "It's about encouraging a culture of continuous learning for everybody and realizing that even though you might be on a board, you don't know everything that you need to know," says Diplock. "There will be other people around the table whose views you respect and listen to and learn from." She recalls how much she took away from chairing a session on "the interoperability of sustainability taxonomies" at the COP26 conference in Glasgow: "That work was fascinating, and I loved what I got from the brilliant minds of the people who were in that group."

Faisal Kazi, Siemens Canada's CEO, highlights the value of reverse mentoring, where board members and senior managers can learn from those they mentor:

> I encourage them to engage in reverse mentoring. I've learned a lot from my mentees. Gen Z and other new generations are much more digitally astute. I learn from their perspective because change is taking place very fast, and if you, as a board member, do not understand what's happening, it can be very tricky. Essentially, as a board member, you have the fiduciary duty to make the best decisions or support the best decisions for the corporation. To do that, you need to embrace lifelong learning.

The world is moving so fast, Kathleen Taylor notes, that "we really need to be recruiting board members who are committed to a constant learning journey. The changes that businesses and boards face are growing exponentially so it's really important to have that continuous learning mindset around the table."

"I'm always impressed when I hear of the board member who comments on learning from educational activities," adds Byron Loflin, Nasdaq's global head of board advisory. "They're actively bringing this knowledge back to other board members, and it's raising their game. What if we had all the board members engaging at that kind of level? Risk evaluation would improve, opportunity identification would improve, and understanding of the company's strategy would improve."

Every board should set aside a training budget, and every board calendar should include a learning opportunity of some kind. In much the same way as lawyers and accountants, boards should disclose the ways in which their members are keeping up to date with the world around them. Many within the Competent Boards network mention their global Competent Boards credentials in governance documents. Some also include relevant qualifications from the US National Association of Corporate Directors and similar bodies in other countries. I believe that such disclosures will become standard practice in the not-too-distant future.

But formal courses and training workshops go only so far. As R. Gopalakrishnan puts it: "You can't play baseball by looking at television. You have to go and hit the ball. And you will realize that in spite of all the television you watched, you're missing the ball each time it comes your way." As valuable as any degree, diploma, or certificate is the determination to serve as a good steward and then act accordingly.

A WIDE-RANGING TRANSITION PLAN

Once the board of the future is in place, it needs to work on a comprehensive transition plan that includes all the elements critical to reinventing the business. This plan must drive positive change as well as address potential risks. In the case of environmental policies, for example, it might include setting emission reduction targets, adopting circular economy principles, and investing in renewable energy sources. Likewise, it could provide for fair labour practices, encourage human rights in the supply chain, and foster diversity and inclusion. "It really depends what's material to the company, understanding that, and then driving long-term value through those plans," says Daouii Abouchere, director of sustainable investing for Europe, the Middle East, and Africa at Wellington Management:

> I know the paperwork is daunting, and it's piling on. But it allows not only investors but also consumers and other companies to measure sustainable performance against peers on a relative and absolute basis. So it's not just talking the talk, but being able to demonstrate how you've integrated these sustainability elements over a long-term time horizon, showcasing year-on-year improvement, and being able to really tell a story behind how sustainability is being integrated and how it's aligning with the firm's values.

LEARNING FROM THE FAMILY BUSINESS

Family-owned businesses are not always a shining example of long-range vision and sound judgment. Many have fallen victim to nepotism, internecine squabbles, and incompetence as younger generations fail to fill the founder's shoes. Even so, the boards of multi-shareholder public companies have much to learn from successful family enterprises.

The best of them—think, for example, of the US's Ideal Industries or India's Tata group—tend to look much further down the road than a couple of quarters or even years. California-based Ideal Industries, now more than a century old and in its fourth generation of family ownership, has a motto that every board would be well advised to emulate: "We see our business in generations, not quarters. This fuels an entrepreneurial culture that creates industry-leading, category-changing products."[67]

Meghan Juday, a governance adviser and family business advocate who also chairs Ideal Industries' board, has some useful advice for the board of the future:

- **Ask questions.** "You want your board to be fiduciary for your shareholders. You want them to be actively asking questions, thinking, understanding their shareholders. Certainly, in a family business that's easier to do than in a public company."

- **Use the talent in the boardroom.** "One of the things that I've noticed in old-style boards is that they have incredible experts and talent in the room, but they never use it. There is never an opportunity for dialogue, for conversation, for access to the network."

- **Get rid of the deadwood.** "A lot of times people get very attached to their directors. They've been there for you. They've supported you. They've helped you be better. It's really hard for someone to step down in the name of service, but one of the most important things is to be very strategic and very open about the skill sets and talents that the business will need."

- **Evaluate directors' performance.** "We do third-party board evaluations. It takes forever, but it's one of the most valuable things we've done."

- **If you're a director, look for feedback.** "If you ask for feedback, chances are you are pretty darn good, right? Because you're self-aware, you're open, you're thinking about it, you want to be of service."

- **Seek out directors who are able and willing to learn.** "One of the things that's really important is whether a director is coachable and open to feedback. I don't want directors who are hard to talk to."

- **Keep learning.** "There are a lot of people who are very valuable, have tons of expertise, and want to give back to the world post-retirement through board service. I think that's great. The risk is allowing your skill set to get a little stale. If you're in a large public company as a senior executive, you don't need extra education because you're literally learning something new every day. It's just so organic. But people forget that when they retire, they have to replace what was once so organic."

WHAT CAN POSSIBLY GO WRONG?

The short answer: Plenty. No matter how thorough the preparatory work and the vetting process, every board is sure to go through some difficult times. We're not talking here about wrong turns by the business but rather about the way the board itself operates. None of us is perfect and we are all attracted to—and repelled by—different personalities. Paul Polman, former Unilever CEO, observes that on far too many boards "there's polite friendship, but it's not a team. Curating these boards is a science as much as an art."

In his book *Toxic Humans: Combatting Poisonous Leadership in Boards and Organizations*, Michael Jenkins describes six types of people, all starting with the letter M, who can quickly turn an effective, congenial board into a dysfunctional one:

- **The Monster,** is, in Jenkins's words, the archetypal narcissistic corporate psychopath. "They are able to put on a show of authentic 'active listening' complete with head nodding and murmuring of assent as they canvass for opinions, but in truth the Monster's mind is made up because [they think their] solution, without question, is the best."

- **The Mouse** is most vulnerable to the groupthink that pervades all too many boardrooms. This type of director "is anxious about being out of [their] depth and so decides to keep a low profile to avoid exposing either [their] lack of knowledge of the business/activities of the organization or [their] inability to deal with complex or complicated issues." Indeed, Jenkins notes, "You might wonder how the Mouse manages to get onto the board in the first place."

- **The Mouth** has little interest in teamwork or in listening to others. "The Mouth has a tendency to be domineering and is completely lacking in self-awareness. Weaker chairs of boards find it a constant battle to grab airtime when they have the Mouth as part of their team. Of course, the situation is even worse if you have two or more Mouths on the same board."

- **The Moaner** is a fixture on most boards, according to Jenkins. "The Moaner will typically lead the way to look at 10 things management has done and then focus on those two items in the list which are still a work in progress and which for very good reasons the team has not yet had a chance to address—and then to complain bitterly and persistently about them (The eight things that have been done well are all but ignored)."

- **The Micromanager** is perhaps the person you least want to have in the future boardroom. As Jenkins puts it: "The Micromanager often has a tragically small worldview. Their weakness as a board member is that their perspectives are too granular and they lack the innovation and creativity to be able to see the bigger picture. Given that one of the roles of a board is to manage risk, the Micromanager is often the one who causes the board to take what they feel is a prudent or safe approach to a potential innovation where the thinking is that it is much better (safer) to put the brakes on something, to stop it outright, than to take an informed, strategic, risk-factored decision."

- **The Muser.** "Sudden intervention by the Muser—which comes with little or no warning—can be the catalyst for chaos. When the Muser decides to speak up, their contribution is more often than not completely left-field, off-beam and off-topic: to call it a distraction for the chair and the rest of the Board is an understatement."

Dear reader, please ask yourself whether you fall into any of Jenkins's toxic categories and, if so, what you can do to become a more collegial and empathetic member of the boardroom team. To guide you in the right direction, here's a list of ten attributes of a great board based on the advice of Leading Governance, a UK-based consultancy:

- Understand your role and responsibilities.

- Lead. Don't manage.

- Engage with others.

- Provide strategic rather than operational support.

- Ensure regular board turnover and succession planning.

- Commit to continuous learning and development.

- Get the right information at board meetings.

- Work as a team.

- Challenge appropriately.

- Review your own performance.[68]

GETTING AHEAD BY GETTING ALONG

Some boards may take the view that in order to adapt to a more complex world, they need to add another member or two, hold a couple of extra meetings each year, or pay board members a bit more for their work. That is undoubtedly the wrong approach. Michael Treschow, former chair of Unilever, asks this trenchant question: "In those companies that have board meetings every month, does the management have time to do anything else? If the culture of a company becomes a meeting culture, that is not a good culture. Either it is poorly organized or people are afraid of taking decisions."

Instead, the board of the future will need to pay more attention to whom it recruits and how its members deal with each other and with the increasingly complex world around them. The skills and personal traits that each director brings to the table mean little if they don't contribute to a vibrant and productive culture, both in the boardroom and in the company at large. No matter what formal controls are in place, the interaction between board and management hinges on open communication channels that everyone, including employees lower down the ladder, can trust.

One way to make that happen, Eric Wetlaufer suggests, is for board members to prioritize asking insightful questions rather than delivering supposedly smart answers:

> It's not about telling senior management how to be innovative. It's about asking where the innovation in the company is and saying: "We want to meet those people. It doesn't matter how young or junior they are; we want to hear from them about how they generate ideas, how resilient those ideas are within the organization, and what obstacles they face."
>
> The board's role is to champion this process by asking questions like: When can we see the new initiatives? What's coming six months from now that we should be aware of today? I don't want to wake up at seven in the morning, open LinkedIn, and see a new company initiative I hadn't heard about before.

With a more diverse group around the table, boards will inevitably find new ways of working. Andrew Howard, head of sustainable investments at the UK-based asset manager Schroders, predicts that directors will need to draw on a wider range of sources for information and that this will inevitably require some adjustment in the way boards and management work together:

> Boards in my experience can vary significantly by the level of interaction they have with the organizations they are overseeing. If it's a case of a dozen people rocking up periodically during the course of the year and having a conversation in a room somewhere and that's the extent of their interaction, that's going to make it quite difficult to get an unfiltered sense of what the issues are that are impacting that industry. It's less about who the specific individuals are around the table, than ultimately ensuring that the information is in front of the people around the table to enable them to make informed decisions.

One critical but often-overlooked dimension of unfiltered communication is a mechanism for employees to make their views known to the board. The director of the future will seize the initiative by meeting as many employees as possible—both junior and senior—in a non-threatening environment, and then using the opportunity to ask probing questions. Any moves by management to discourage such contacts should be viewed with suspicion. Furthermore, the board should ensure that a trusted mechanism is in place for whistle-blowers to be heard with the seriousness and confidentiality they deserve.

When it comes to whistle-blowers, "it's important that people know that these things are taken seriously by the board," says Claudia Sender Ramirez, a director of the Brazilian aircraft maker Embraer and several other multinationals. "When we interact with employees, when we go on factory visits or customer visits, they should know that we address this issue in the same way as we talk about employee health and safety or customer care." At the same time, members of the future board should make it their business to involve employees as far as possible in forums and other discussions on topics like cybercrime, thereby encouraging them to find new ways of protecting the company.

Sender Ramirez says that one of her boards seeks to engender this kind of culture by taking fifteen minutes or so at the start of every meeting for a discussion on compliance. "Because compliance also evolves, right?" she notes. "Things that were accepted in the past are not accepted anymore today, and there are so many grey areas. I think that for the whole organization, knowing that the board dedicates time at every meeting to discuss compliance is a really big thing."

Compliance may be necessary, but it is far from sufficient. In my discussions with corporate governance experts on the qualities most likely to be sought after in the board of the future, one that crops up repeatedly is *courage*, or, as Katell Le Goulven, executive director of INSEAD'S Hoffmann Institute, describes it: courage beyond compliance. That means the courage to question fellow directors, management, and other employees, as well as outsiders such as activists, analysts, suppliers, and customers.

Gopalakrishnan defines courage around the boardroom table this way:

> Courage is the ability to break through the behavioural and psychological pressures that a director faces. It's the ability to use your own judgment, make inquiries, not get cowed by the fact that you're not an expert in the field. Everyone on the board feels that it should be collegial. You should be good buddies. You might have played golf together last weekend. I have no problem with that. My problem is when you fail to address a question that's rankling in your mind because everybody else has said yes to it. So you just say yes.
>
> Courage is the ability to state your point of view and stick to it—and yet be open in case somebody is trying to persuade you, because not all persuasion is illegitimate or misdirected.

Kathleen Taylor elaborates:

> Directors are there as stewards of the shareholders, so we need to be thinking about our place in stewarding an organization, supporting management, and when necessary bringing challenges and asking tough questions. That can always be respectfully done in ways that are very helpful to management.

Daouii Abouchere highlights the importance of the board working in tandem with senior management on corporate strategy in general and sustainability in particular. "It's not just the C-suite in isolation or the board driving a mandate," Abouchere says, emphasizing:

> It's the alignment of the board of directors and the C-suite together in driving change. Many companies are doing it

really well, and it's always the ones which have that strong linkage between the board and the C-suite, and being able to effectively showcase that.

The most powerful sustainability teams collaborate effectively with finance and accounting, risk management and compliance, helping to identify the financial significance of ESG factors. Quantifying the dollar impact of these factors on the company's financial performance helps boardrooms prioritize and allocate resources effectively.

Andrew Howard neatly encapsulates the transition from the board of the past to the board of the future: "It's about information flows and equipping people who are around the table to make informed decisions on a bigger range of areas than was perhaps the case in a world where a dozen people got together periodically, had a bit of a chat for a while, and then went home after a nice lunch."

///

Ten Questions for the Board of the Future

1. What are two types of training that you have signed up for in the past two years that have made you a more effective and competent board member?

2. Can you name a time in the past year or two that you have informally collaborated with another board member for the benefit of the company?

3. Which newspapers and other media do you follow and/or subscribe to? Do they present different points of view?

4. Do you talk too much at board meetings? Or do you make a point of listening to your colleagues?

5. Does the expertise around your boardroom table sufficiently reflect your company's business and the issues facing it?

6. What value does each of your fellow directors bring to your board?

7. Does your company have a policy in place to protect authentic whistle-blowers?

8. When you meet senior executives, do you tend to ask questions or dispense advice?

9. Can you name a time when you have shown courage beyond compliance in your board work?

10. How often do you and your colleagues express disagreement with the company's chief executive during a board meeting?

CHAPTER SIX

Who Should Be at the Future Boardroom Table?

I'm a big fan of boardroom diversity because the world is diverse. There's a lot going on, and the more experiences you have around the table, the better off you are. And it's just fun dealing with people from different backgrounds and different areas of expertise.

—Robert Herz, former chairman of the US Financial Accounting Standards Board

If there's one prediction that members of the Competent Boards network unanimously agree on, it's this: the board of the future will look very different from the board of today. The reason is simple. There's a growing realization that a diversity of views around the boardroom table leads to more invigorating discussions and, as a result, smarter decisions and better performance. And the only way of eliciting that diversity of views is by recruiting directors from the widest possible range of backgrounds relevant to the company's business, whether measured by age, race, sexual orientation, geographical origins, cultural background, or business experience. We need those diverse minds to rethink attitudes and strategies that were once considered the norm, but no longer serve the best interests of either the company or society.

Our understanding of diversity in the boardroom is undergoing a sea change. The term has long been confined to attributes such as gender presentation, age, and race. While these remain important, future diversity initiatives will increasingly emphasize deeper dimensions, such as cognitive diversity, familiarity with different cultures, and life experiences.

This shift recognizes that true diversity goes beyond appearance and includes diverse ways of thinking, solving problems, and understanding the world around us. Thus, cognitive diversity refers to the inclusion of individuals who bring different perspectives and approaches to problem-solving, a critical element in fostering innovation and creativity. In practice, this means that the board of the future will seek members with more varied educational backgrounds, professional experiences, and ways of thinking.

I can't put the case for boardroom diversity more eloquently than Annette Bak Kirby, a top team effectiveness and boardroom coach based in Abu Dhabi:

> It is perfectly fine to have tensions in the boardroom. It is how we deal with them that determines the quality of our collective decision-making. The chair sets the tone for the boardroom being a safe space for high-quality conversations. When board members have the ability to listen well, step beyond their own firmly held positions, and ask questions from a place of curiosity rather than opposition, that's when they elevate the quality of decision-making. Such a shift in behaviour requires inner maturity of board members so they can effectively embrace tensions through diversity of thought in dealing with the complexity of today's boardroom challenges.

A POWERFUL TOOL FOR TRANSFORMATION

Board diversity should never be a check-the-box compliance exercise designed to fulfill quotas or satisfy activists. Rather, the aim must be to recruit the best people to guide—and, if necessary, transform—the company. As it happens, diversity can be a powerful tool to make that happen. Decision-making is indisputably elevated by being able to draw on the widest variety of talent available. By confining the search process to a limited pool of candidates (whether men, women, baby boomers, or whatever), a board risks depriving itself of people who may have a valuable contribution to make in today's fast-moving, unpredictable world.

Paul Polman, Unilever's former chief executive, says that broadening diversity should be one of the most urgent tasks for anyone seeking to rejuvenate a tired board:

> Everybody wants someone on the board that understands AI or technology, and there simply aren't enough people out there. So I don't envy boards. But you have to ask yourself: Are we changing fast enough? And I would say that very few boards could answer that in the affirmative. Or, if they are changing, it often is not necessarily in the right direction.
>
> I would have a deliberate strategy, very fast, to look at board composition. Think about who represents planet earth, think about how we can represent future generations. Think creatively about what a different board looks like, what diversity looks like, that goes beyond skill or colour of skin or gender. Then invest much more in hooking up boards with the external environment. Don't have the board meetings in the office, meet somewhere else, invite other people in, create oxygen.

HOW TO MAKE THE RIGHT CHOICES

Francesca Ecsery, who serves on five boards including that of Air France, makes the point that diversity—like many other corporate goals—can often be achieved in small but consistent steps. She cites the example of a major US retailer whose board for years resisted outside pressure to stop selling tobacco products because they made such a huge contribution to the bottom line. It was not until three women had been appointed to the board and forcefully made the case for change that the company agreed to change tack. What's more, implementing the decision took four or five years. "As a non-executive director, you don't have the levers to change everything overnight," Ecsery says, "but with the right culture, the right vision, the right people on the board, and with good diversity of thinking, you can get there eventually."

The starting point must be a board that reflects the communities that the business serves. That means recruiting directors who not only fit the board's skills matrix but also have their fingers on the pulse of the various constituencies important to the business today and, even more important, in the future. A company planning to expand into Latin America, for example, would be wise to have a Brazilian or Chilean or Peruvian on its board, probably with some experience in its particular sector. However, I believe that generalists tend to make more effective directors than people with a narrow field of expertise, no matter how impressive that expertise may be. They must be willing to forge and maintain relationships with a wide range of stakeholder groups. It doesn't take a genius to know that the more comfortable stakeholders feel talking to a board, the more likely that their interaction will produce useful feedback and fresh ideas.

IT'S TIME FOR TERM LIMITS

It is hard to dispute the criticism that the vast majority of corporate boards are, to put it bluntly, too old. The retirement age of directors on S&P 500 boards averaged 74 in 2024, unchanged for four years, according to a Spencer Stuart survey.[69] The average age of directors of public companies has steadily crept *up* over the past few decades, reaching 63.5 years for S&P 500 companies in 2023.[70] That's the age most people start thinking of retirement, and many have already moved on to the land of golf courses and grandchildren. What's more, the average age of new directors was not much lower, at 58.2 years.

"I believe people are sitting too long on boards," says Michael Treschow, former chair of Unilever, which has a policy of replacing at least one board member every year. Treschow notes that under UK rules, directors are not considered independent if they have served on a board for longer than nine years. As a result, Unilever and numerous other companies limit tenure to a maximum of nine years. "A well-organized succession plan is then to plan ahead so not too many leave at the same time," says Treschow. The goal is thus to have one or two new directors each year. Former Bank of America and Royal Dutch Shell chair Chad Holliday is another fan of term limits. He says that when he joins a board, one of the first things he looks for is whether any of his fellow directors "are just hanging around."

The standard argument in favour of silver-haired directors has been that boards benefit from the experience and wisdom that come with age. While there may be some truth in that, the limitations of baby boomers and the benefits of younger voices at the table have never been more obvious. Younger generations are far more attuned than their parents or grandparents to the threats facing humankind from climate change, pollution, and income inequality. People in their twenties, thirties, and forties represent the consumers, employees, and investors of tomorrow, precisely the constituencies that every business should be setting its sights on.

What's more, few men and women over sixty—much less seventy—can claim to be more in touch than Gen Xers and Gen Zers with the fast-evolving digital technology that now pervades the business world. The young dominate the worlds of cybersecurity, artificial intelligence, quantum computing, blockchain, and social media, to mention a few. "Yesterday's experience is not necessarily the best experience for this brave new world that we're facing," says Jane Diplock, supervisory board member of the World Benchmarking Alliance and a former director of the Singapore Exchange.

Claudia Sender Ramirez, a director of Embraer and several other multinationals, adds that colleagues from non-business backgrounds, such as academia, "bring us a point of view that we wouldn't have had otherwise."

Even so, Holliday makes the point that term limits are as relevant for young directors as for older ones: "It's very helpful to have some thirty-year-olds coming on boards who know the newer technologies and are more in touch with things that are going on. And yet, you also wouldn't want them serving for forty years. If you bring in somebody when they're forty and you have a mandatory retirement age of seventy-two, that's a long run. It's just not healthy to keep people on a board that long. They get lazy."

Some encouraging signs of change are emerging. The average tenure of US board directors has fallen from 8.6 years in 2013 to 7.8 in 2023.[71] In India, 13.9 percent of directors of companies listed on the National Stock Exchange were younger than 45 towards the end of 2023, up from 10.9 percent a decade earlier.[72] Some companies have begun setting term limits for board members, while others have adopted mandates for age diversity. Spencer Stuart reports that the proportion of S&P 500 boards with a mandatory retirement age of seventy-five or older doubled (from 30 to 60 percent) between 2014 and 2024.

Thankfully, the message seems to be sinking in that the board of the future must be younger than its predecessors. While that is certainly the right way to go, some words of caution are in order. As older board members step down in greater numbers, there is a danger that those who replace them will be so eager at the prospect of a board appointment that they will fail to do the necessary due diligence. In the process, they run the risk of taking the blame for their predecessors' shortcomings as skeletons start falling out of the closet. Conversely, the board may get less than it hoped for if the newcomers arrive without their eyes open and a mindset to get to work.

NEW DEFINITIONS OF DIVERSITY

As the search for younger faces shows, the board of the future will need to think of diversity in hitherto unfamiliar ways.

"Diversity doesn't necessarily mean gender and age," says Michael Treschow. "It really means diversity of minds, diversity of skills and experience needed in the business, so you can look 360 degrees around the business and cover all the bases."

Increasingly, boards will look to recruit a wider range of skills and personalities than in the past. That also means different mindsets. "I'd like to see people who are risk averse merged in with people who are not so risk averse because that discussion is critical," says Maali Khader, chief executive of the Middle East Institute of Directors. "I'd like to see more diversity, more conversation, more comfort in discussing and disagreeing on issues. People are still not comfortable enough to say: 'I disagree. I come from a different school of thought. I see things differently.'"

Another facet of diversity seldom mentioned in the context of corporate boards is appropriate representation of people with disabilities, even though 16 percent of the world's population lives with a disability. The Valuable 500, a group of five hundred chief executives from high-profile companies and organizations around the world, was formed in 2019 by Competent Boards network member Caroline Casey to advance disability inclusion within their own workplaces and to put the issue on their board agendas.[73]

But seeking a range of views and backgrounds should not necessarily mean adding a specialist in X and another specialist in Y to the board. A point made repeatedly in this book is that the director of the future is less likely to be an expert in a specific field than a person of the world with a broad understanding of the issues shaping the environment in which a particular business operates.

Andrew Howard, global head of sustainable investments at Schroders, elaborates:

> It's a bit more of a nuanced question than asking: Is there a climate scientist on the board? Is there somebody who has a clear background in the science of a particular topic? That's probably not the right outcome in most cases. Ultimately, we're looking for organizational skill sets around the table and a board of directors working in the way that effective boards do, which is having diverse opinions from different perspectives and armed with enough knowledge to bring challenge and perspective to different topics. It's more about broad-based knowledge as it's relevant to the company and the industry than about, for example, climate science. That doesn't necessarily mean that everyone around the table needs to be an expert in everything. It does mean that individuals are armed with enough information and enough perspective to challenge as appropriate for that business.

WHAT EXPERTISE IS NEEDED?

Board members, especially at large public companies, are invariably smart, well-meaning individuals with a wealth of experience. However, they all too often come from very similar backgrounds, which means that the board as a whole tends to have a limited view of the world around it—to the detriment of the business.

Byron Loflin, Nasdaq's head of board advisory, recalls that he once asked Jay Lorsch, a professor of human relations at Harvard Business School, how Lorsch would rate the average board member. "D-plus," was Lorschs's spontaneous reply. However, it's not quite that clear-cut, Loflin argues: "I believe mostly A-level people are engaged on boards, but they're producing B-level or lower results." A big reason for that underperformance is that too many board members are recruited mainly for their financial experience, giving them a valuable but limited set of skills. Instead, Loflin says, boards should be asking: "What other expertise is needed, and what does that expertise and cognitive diversity contribute to the boardroom?" He elaborates:

> Committee structuring and responsibility should be reassessed to verify that enough people have the skills, the diversity of experience, and the cognitive diversity to address the speed and breadth of today's needs. So, as we go around the room, the people are probably going to look very different, because we have a highly diverse society, particularly in North America. A central question for CEOs, chairs, and investors is: Is this board adding value to total shareholder return and stakeholder advantages, for example, talent attraction?
>
> The boardroom shouldn't look just like me, because I have only a narrow set of skills and experience in my life. There should be, as it is on average, ten different people working together in that important collegial way where they're pushing back and offering insights. But, historically, the level of knowledge and engagement has drifted lower. The best boards are raising the bar so that board members bring more of their full selves, that they are taking the expertise that they have and wrestling and massaging it intellectually in other areas of life, and bringing it back to the boardroom.

The Competent Boards future boardroom survey underscores both the desire and the need for more diversity. More than three-quarters of respondents anticipate a move away from token representation towards a genuine variety of people around the boardroom table. Two-thirds of respondents foresee boards becoming more inclusive of a range of stakeholder perspectives, including different markets, cultures, and age groups that align with their companies' values and purpose. One insightful participant urges companies to put less emphasis on the raw statistics of board diversity, and to focus instead on reporting the qualities that directors from different backgrounds bring to the table. I completely agree. We should not just be reporting raw diversity statistics and the number of meetings that each director attends. What really matters is that we have a well-functioning boardroom enriched by diverse points of view, mutual respect, and an eagerness to find the best solutions for the company after all have shared their varying perspectives.

OBSTACLES REMAIN

But there is a problem. No matter how well-intentioned and far-sighted the Competent Boards network and our survey respondents may be, the push for diversity still faces resistance in many quarters. As Tensie Whelan, director of New York University's Stern Center for Sustainable Business, observes:

> You have entrenched systems, people who are very happy
> with their paycheque and staying where they are for as long
> as possible, who don't necessarily have the expertise or even
> the passion or interest in these new topics. I've had women

tell me, "Yeah, I met with the chairman. And clearly I was just there so he could say he reviewed a bunch of women, but he ended up bringing on one of his male buddies."

There needs to be real commitment by the executive leadership and board leadership to diversify the board over time to bring in more skill sets. That becomes the business of the nominating committee, and they need to set targets for that.

Whelan also highlights the risk of tokenism:

We need to avoid the trap where you put a woman or a black person on the board and expect them to be the voice for all women and all black people. Similarly, you can't put a chief sustainability officer on the board and expect that person to be the voice for all sustainability issues. You need to have education and engagement so that one or two or even three people out of a fifteen-member board can help catalyze the full board. If they're seen as having been brought in to deal with women's issues or renewables, they'll be marginalized just to those issues. That's not what we want. These issues need to be mainstreamed. Having those diverse voices supported by the ethos and governance of the board can make a real difference in outcomes.

Regrettably, the issue of workplace diversity has been drawn into the current "culture wars" in the US. As politicians take aim at the DEI movement for promoting "wokeness," businesses have become more wary of expanding diversity initiatives. Employers have also been swayed by the June 2023 Supreme Court ruling that struck down race-based affirmative action programs at Harvard University and the University of North Carolina.[74] Although the parties to the case were universities, businesses have become fearful that the court's decision could spark legal challenges to their own diversity programs. Indeed, within a month of the Harvard and UNC ruling, attorneys general in thirteen Republican-controlled states sent a letter to the chief executives of Fortune 100 companies warning that their diversity, equity, and inclusion hiring practices might be illegal.[75] (On the other hand, more than twenty Democratic attorneys general told the same companies just the opposite, reassuring them that these programs reduce the risk of anti-discrimination suits.)

Given this less welcoming environment, it is hardly surprising that a string of well-known companies, including Walmart, Ford Motor, John Deere, and Harley-Davidson, have rolled back their DEI policies.[76] Netflix, Walt Disney, and Warner Bros. Discovery, among others, have announced the departure of high-profile diversity, equity and inclusion executives.[77] In BlackRock's 2025 proxy voting guidelines, gender, race, and ethnic diversity is described as "a mix of professional and personal characteristics that is comparable to market norms." BlackRock's 2025 proxy voting guidelines note that

> appropriately qualified, engaged directors with characteristics relevant to a company's business enhance the ability of the board to add value and be the voice of shareholders in board discussions ... We are interested in a variety of experiences, perspectives, and skill sets in the boardroom. We see it as a means of promoting diversity of thought to avoid "group think" in the board's exercise of its responsibilities to advise and oversee management ... We look for companies to explain how their approach to board composition supports the company's governance practices.[78, 79]

Robert Herz, former chairman of the US Financial Accounting Standards Board, succinctly sums up the benefits of a diverse board, no matter what the political climate outside the boardroom:

> People with different experiences enrich the whole tapestry of the board. You want people that have the personal traits of being able to work in a decision-making environment that respects other people and who learn, listen, and are willing to be very curious and challenging and probing. I've seen that evolve over the past fifteen to twenty years and even more so in the last ten years, with both a greater diversity of board members in terms of backgrounds and experiences, and also in the way boards operate.

Joyce Cacho, who chairs Sistema Biobolsa and serves on several other boards, goes even further:

> The time has arrived for boardroom composition to be looked at as a risk. If boardrooms don't look like the markets that companies currently serve or groups of people who are in their strategic growth plans, as a manufacturer or a service provider, then, literally, your boardroom composition is a risk factor. Data and evidence are publicly available showing that when you have more systematically under-represented communities, especially women with steelplate defying career paths, in the boardroom, businesses perform with less volatility and more solid growth.
>
> Boardroom composition that stagnates with "tradition" is where risk lies because it signals to investors and consumers that there is misalignment between the words of marketing and communication, and core business strategy. This leaves

questions about company alignment unanswered and/or confusingly answered.

The time will soon come, I believe, when the benefits of diversity are so obvious that shareholders insist on appointing board members who understand the stakeholders that their companies serve today and want to serve in the future.

///

Ten Questions for the Board of the Future

1. Can you name three ways in which the makeup of your board reflects the diverse views of your company's employees and the communities where it does business?

2. Are there any relevant constituencies that you think are not well understood by the board? By the same token, are any stakeholder groups too much in focus?

3. What is the average age of the members of your board?

4. Are any of your board members under the age of forty-five? If not, why not?

5. Does your board consider diversity when considering candidates for vacant posts? If so, what kind of diversity and why?

6. When disagreements arise at your board meetings, do the alternative views always come from the same people?

7. If so, why do you think other board members do not speak up?

8. Can you name three things you have learned from fellow board members who come from different backgrounds from yourself?

9. Do you think your board will look different in ten years from the way it looks today with respect to competencies, including hard skills and soft skills? If so, in what way?

10. Does your board have a plan to broaden its diversity and transform to a board of choice?

CHAPTER SEVEN

Technology: Master or Servant?

Helping management think through and forecast the unintended consequences of the technologies that we're embracing and how we're deploying them is, for sure, a role of the board.

—Claudia Sender Ramirez, director, Embraer, Telefónica, and Holcim

It's 2029 and the directors of the world's largest electric-vehicle maker, GTCM, are gathered around a boardroom table in Shanghai, each wearing an earpiece and a wireless mic on their lapels. In front of them is a small silver box adorned with the corporate logo, a stylized flash of lightning spanning the globe. The box is an artificial intelligence device stuffed with data on every aspect of GTCM's operations: its financial statements, its suppliers around the world, its dealerships, the buyers of its cars, and much more. Instead of talking to each other or to the senior managers in attendance, the directors spend much of the meeting peppering the chatbot with questions and listening to its responses, given in any one of eight languages in a voice as clear as a human being's. The chatbot not only provides information but sketches different scenarios, describing the outcomes that flow from different assumptions. It outlines potential benefits and risks, then recommends the best way to proceed. Before the meeting wraps up, it summarizes the discussion and suggests how the various agenda items can be synthesized into formal motions for approval. The directors depart for their post-meeting dinner, well satisfied with their—or to be more accurate, the chatbot's—work.

Is this how the board meeting of the future will unfold, with the most valuable insights coming not from a human being but from a machine? Some companies are already moving in that direction. As long ago as 2014 a Hong Kong venture capital firm, Deep Knowledge Ventures, appointed VITAL, machine learning software, to its board of directors.[80] The firm's managing partner said that no investment decisions would be made without a green light from VITAL. The question for all board members is: Should a "robo-director" have a seat at the boardroom table?

Since VITAL's groundbreaking appointment, it has become all but obvious that advanced technology will play an invaluable role in the boardroom of the future—with far-reaching implications, for both better and worse. Tools such as artificial intelligence, machine learning, augmented reality, and quantum computing, among many others, have the potential to make an enormous contribution to the productivity of boards and the quality of their decisions. But they also pose some serious risks.

In this chapter, we examine both the benefits and the threats of this digital revolution, as well as how the board of the future can take advantage of the former while mitigating the latter. The bottom line is that the way boards use AI and other digital tools could turn out to be a critical determinant of a company's long-term success and, by extension, its directors' reputations.

THE REWARDS

As in many other walks of life, the digital revolution is driving dramatic changes in boardrooms around the world. Artificial intelligence in particular holds the promise of a vast commercial payback by improving efficiency, reducing costs, and enhancing decision-making capabilities. Goldman Sachs estimated in 2023 that advances in natural language processing could boost global output by nearly 7 percent and productivity by 1.5 percentage points over the next decade, at least partially automating two-thirds of current occupations.[81] Yet an IBM Institute for Business Value survey in late 2024 found that while 77 percent of executives say they need to adopt generative AI quickly to keep up with their competitors, only a quarter strongly agree that their organization's IT infrastructure can support expanding AI across the enterprise.[82] As IBM points out, "In this environment, leaders are walking a tightrope between agility and security, striking a balance between resilience and risk. It's no easy feat."

Given these findings, we can expect an escalating demand for AI-related skills in boardrooms and executive suites. Respondents to the Competent Boards future boardroom survey overwhelmingly believe that AI will play a pivotal role in future boardroom dynamics through risk management, decision support, and strategic considerations. AI will percolate to every corner of business, making itself felt in ways as diverse as supply-chain management, simplifying contracts, and tracking greenwashing claims along a company's entire supply chain.

AI will empower boards to move beyond traditional measurements of success like quarterly financial forecasts. Advanced analytics can quickly synthesize data on the impact of specific assumptions, policies, and outcomes, helping to build plausible scenarios and stress-test different options by using digital twins. Done properly, this shift will give board members a more comprehensive and dynamic understanding of what's being measured, leading to more informed discussion and—hopefully—wiser decisions.

AI can also be put to work to streamline processes in areas like compliance management, allowing lawyers and other professionals to focus on seizing new opportunities in their various fields. To take one example, several prominent banks, including Danske Bank, Credit Suisse, Santander Bank, USAA Federal Savings Bank, and Wells Fargo, have explored the use of AI and machine learning to improve compliance with US money laundering regulations. All these institutions have found themselves in the crosshairs of regulators in recent years, paying a combined US$2.2 billion for various regulatory infractions. Recognizing AI's potential as a tool to combat money laundering, they have harnessed a system known as federated machine learning, a form of AI that preserves data privacy by keeping sensitive data on local servers while allowing globally applicable analysis.[83]

Technology can even play a powerful role in promoting board diversity, a critical issue for the board of the future discussed in the previous chapter. Digital collaboration tools and virtual meeting applications, such as Zoom and Microsoft Teams, have made it much easier to tap into the varying talents and perspectives of directors in different parts of the world. More than that, they enable people with disabilities or who live in remote communities to communicate in ways that were unheard of just a few years ago.

Daouii Abouchere, Wellington Management's director of sustainable investing for Europe, the Middle East, and Africa, vividly describes the vast potential of AI and other forms of technology to help boards and their companies improve efficiency as well as sustainability:

> It's the ability to be able to really grasp data and understand data without having to spend hours toggling through chunky Excels and finding patterns. If done properly, AI can be harnessed as a positive tool for sustainability integration. The more you can see down your supply chain, the better. Integrating and adopting successful AI strategies helps boardrooms to be proactive in their engagement with stakeholders, to understand the concerns and expectations of those stakeholders, and then mapping it to the data and seeing where there are opportunities for improvement in the processes.
>
> Examples include implementing smart sensors and Internet of Things devices to monitor energy consumption and reduce waste in production processes. Big data analytics are employed to identify patterns and trends in supply chain operations, allowing for better risk management and identification of potential environmental and social impacts.

We also see AI-driven algorithms utilized to optimize transportation and logistics where we're minimizing the carbon footprint of distribution networks.

The integration of technology with sustainability is showcasing tangible benefits for both the environment and the business. My favourite example is a global retail company that streamlines its supply chain using AI, resulting in reduced transportation emissions and costs, and allowing it to effectively map out its product use and create a more circular environment. On top of that, it can add AI to its customer identification and trend patterns, so only making the stock that is required rather than mass-producing and overproducing. AI and technology, if used efficiently, can help us not only see the data, but also manage excessive waste, ensure efficiency, and reduce companies' overall environmental impact on the planet.

Abouchere's perspective is just one of many that I have heard from Competent Boards network members around the world. The list of potential benefits from AI is truly almost endless.

THE RISKS

Whatever their technological wizardry, AI models also pose significant risks that no board dare overlook. Confidentiality, accuracy disruption, and a lack of nuance are among the main concerns that boards of the future should be aware of. "Whatever you put into an external AI tool becomes part of the public database," notes Kathleen Taylor, chair of Element Fleet Management and former Royal Bank of Canada chair. "So in the race to adopt AI, companies and directors should be asking the question: Do we have the right guardrails around the use of external AI tools in our business so that we're taking full advantage of the power of the technology but not giving up trade secrets and confidential information?" Likewise, she adds, "Anyone who has used ChatGPT or another similar tool knows that while it might be extremely accurate in sending me the top six restaurants in the city, it can make mistakes on topics that are more subjective or complicated."

Unlike the humans who sit around a board table, AI models have no legal liability for the consequences of their actions. Generative AI learns from past interactions, so the outputs and responses it provides are based on what has happened in days, months, and years gone by. While the latest versions of predictive AI can help us look into the future, they cannot (yet) match the ability of the human brain to dissect and interpret the twists, turns, and nuances that may come into play in the boardroom. In other words, artificial intelligence is no substitute for the sound judgment and common sense that rational human beings bring to the table. But it might be valuable as a co-pilot.

Claudia Sender Ramirez, a director of several Brazilian and European companies, adds that boards and senior executives need to consider not only the direct risks of AI but also the unintended (and often unanticipated) consequences that can flow from bias and ethical lapses. Drawing a lesson from social media, she notes, "I don't think that when Instagram was developed, they were thinking 'Oh, we're going to get teenage girls depressed.'"

These risks and shortcomings mean that the board of the future must have the foresight to make sure that it is using

AI to its advantage, and not being manipulated by it. Board members will need to probe the potential for unintended consequences and trust their own judgment and common sense. True, they are expected to do much the same today, but even the smartest human beings can easily be intimidated if all the world's accumulated knowledge appears to suggest a course of action that differs from what their own instincts are telling them.

Retired Tata Sons executive director R. Gopalakrishnan compares the current state of AI to the early days of nuclear science, in the sense that most people's ignorance of the technology still far exceeds their knowledge. He notes:

> You must let the technology develop, you cannot suppress it. But you must always be curious about its downside, whereas the techie will give you the upside. Directors should have a healthy skepticism towards artificial intelligence rather than buying into it. Directors should be humble enough and smart enough to say: "I don't understand" and "What can go wrong if we did this?"

ETHICS LOOM LARGE

Any discussion of artificial intelligence at the boardroom table would not be complete without considering the numerous—and often thorny—ethical issues involved in its use. No fewer than 80 percent of respondents to the Competent Boards future boardroom survey recognize the urgency of integrating ethical considerations into the use of AI, and almost three-quarters anticipate a substantial integration of ethics into boardroom policies and discussions on AI. At the same time, AI model designers are increasingly aware of the need to align AI with principles of inclusivity and belonging.

Privacy should be near if not at the top of the board's concerns. AI, especially in technologies like virtual reality, can potentially capture and misuse personal information of customers or employees. It's imperative for boards to ensure that privacy norms continue to be enforced and that necessary approvals are obtained, especially during the data collection and processing stages.

Bias, whether deliberate or unconscious and often reflecting prevailing prejudices, can easily seep into AI models. This is particularly concerning in AI applications related to personnel recruiting, lending, research and development, or any other activity where decisions have a direct impact on people's lives. Boards must prioritize the development of fair AI systems and ensure that they are tested for biases and fairness. They also have a duty to ensure that the use of AI conforms to the organization's mission and values. That means setting out a framework that defines the ethical use of data and ensuring that all adhere to it. On another front, the use of AI must be transparent and explainable in plain language if a company is to maintain the trust of its stakeholders.

Ethics guidelines have little credibility if they are not subject to continuous monitoring and accountability. In today's fast-moving world, perceptions of what is ethical and what is not are evolving, and boards should put processes in place to keep abreast of the times. Finally, there should be clear provisions for cutting loose a technology tool that veers away from the ethical or operational standards set by the board.

Joyce Cacho, a veteran independent director in global manufacturing and banking, notes that the ethical use of technology is especially critical in today's polarized society:

> We have access to enormous amounts of data about employees and customers alike, and it's hard to claim ignorance with the proliferation of public data. We can't say we didn't know something when that information is readily available with a few clicks or even a voice command on our handheld devices.
>
> How companies handle this readily accessible data, how they ensure they're not letting their biases influence its usage, is a significant challenge. It's especially critical because we're currently experiencing a low point in trust—interpersonal trust, trust between corporations and society, and trust between society and politics.

Ensuring high ethical standards in the application of technology will add to the board's workload. But the effort is sure to be worthwhile if it fosters responsible AI use, builds trust among stakeholders, and mitigates risks. It is undoubtedly worth the effort to ensure that technology is used ethically rather than taking the risk of a blunder down the road that ends up causing heavy financial costs, not to mention reputational damage. IBM's chief technology officer Khwaja Shaik has a blunt word of advice: "If you don't have an AI ethics board today, establish it right now."

FROM SECURITY TO RESILIENCE

Barely a week passes without news of a cyberattack on a prominent business, utility, hospital, or government department somewhere in the world. In 2022, researchers at the University of Queensland in Australia concluded that "boards are not nearly as engaged in cybersecurity as they are in other areas of oversight."[84] That still appeared to be the case two years later, when a 2024 Diligent and Bitsight survey of more than four thousand mid-sized and large companies around the world found that only 5 percent had a cybersecurity specialist on their board.[85] Clearly, boards need to pay far more attention to this issue.

IBM estimated in its annual *Cost of a Data Breach Report 2024* that the average total cost of a cyberattack, based on a survey of 604 organizations, reached an all-time high of US$4.88 million in the year to March 2024, up 10 percent from the previous year and the highest total ever.[86] The survey estimated that organizations that used security AI and automation to prevent attacks saved an average of US$2.2 million compared to those that took no such precautionary measures. Meantime, ransomware payments surged to record highs in 2024. *Security Intelligence* estimated that in the first half of the year, victims paid US$459.8 million to cybercriminals.[87] The largest single ransom payment ever revealed was US$75 million paid to the Dark Angels ransomware group by an undisclosed Fortune 50 company. More than half of the respondents to IBM's survey said they were planning to boost security investments as a result of a breach, with a focus on incident response, planning and testing, employee training, and threat detection and response technologies.

The damage caused by cyberattacks often goes far beyond dollars and cents. "Compelling evidence demonstrates how successful cyber-breaches translate into unexpected negative shocks to a firm's reputation, adversely affecting the stock market activity and hampering the wealth of share-/ stakeholders," the University of Queensland study noted. This concern is underlined by rules adopted by the US Securities and Exchange Commission that enhance and standardize the disclosure of cybersecurity risk management, strategy, governance, and incident reporting.[88] Any board worth its salt should be paying attention.

Responsibility for cybersecurity cannot be left to the IT department, which seldom reports to the chief executive, much less to the board of directors. It is an issue that affects an entire business, and every board should be taking steps to ensure that its company is equipped to meet the threat. As Khwaja Shaik sees it, the board has three critical roles:

- Providing the oversight that enables business success. In other words, the board needs to ensure that cybersecurity is integrated into the company's business strategy.

- Considering and guiding risk appetite, profile, and tolerance, which means setting out a clear risk policy and deciding what risks the company is willing to take.

- Promoting a culture and strategic direction that give cybersecurity the priority it deserves and deliver value for the money invested in it.

Shaik adds:

> As board directors, we must evolve beyond viewing cybersecurity as purely a risk management function. Our oversight should focus on how security investments directly contribute to revenue growth, customer trust, and employee

experience. Show me the metrics that demonstrate this value creation.

The new SEC cybersecurity disclosure requirements aren't just a compliance exercise—they're an opportunity to reshape our security operating model. We need to build security into our business DNA, ensuring our disclosures reflect a mature, business-aligned security program that investors can trust.

The partnership between security and finance is critical. The audit committee working closely with the chief financial officer helps us strike the right balance between protecting assets and enabling growth. Every security dollar spent should yield measurable business returns, whether through risk reduction, operational efficiency, or competitive advantage.

While the vast majority of respondents to the Competent Boards future boardroom survey say they expect boards to place a heavier emphasis on cybersecurity, the question of how this should be done is a matter of vigorous debate. Some governance experts prefer to give primary responsibility to the audit committee, others to the risk committee. Some boards have set up a specific cybersecurity committee.

Dottie Schindlinger, executive director of the Diligent Institute, is among those who believe that boards should shift the emphasis from cybersecurity to the more proactive concept of cyber-resilience. She explains:

Just assume that you're going to have a problem and practice how you will respond. Practice how quickly you will shut it down, how you will protect people, how you will communicate with them. If anything has happened to their stuff or to their trust, just practice that. I feel that if you just focus on cyber-resilience, you're probably going to be okay.

Siemens Canada's Faisal Kazi emphasizes the importance of involving technology-savvy young people in board decisions on these topics: "Whatever course a board chooses to take, it is crucial to involve next-generation talent who are adept with technology because they have a different way of thinking and handling things."

Each course of action has pros and cons but the bottom line is that, in the words of CPA Canada, one of the world's largest national accounting organizations, "the board has a responsibility to include cybersecurity as an essential skill within the board's skills matrix, and to populate the board accordingly."[89] One common thread, CPA Canada's chief executive Pamela Steer notes, is that "it is advisable to have a range of cyber skills spread across multiple directors rather than rely on only one person to interpret cybersecurity reports."

THE UNDERBELLY OF THE DIGITAL AGE

It has taken a while, but boards are at last waking up to the realization that business is not immune to the malevolent actors who have infiltrated the digital revolution. The rumours, conspiracy theories, and manipulated material that they produce have tangible consequences. They can seriously damage a company's brand and reputation, leading to a loss of stakeholder trust, and real—although sometimes hard to measure—financial loss. And, as we all know, it is far easier to spread fake news than to correct it or squelch it. In one early case, Coca-Cola was the victim of a false story on social media in 2017 that claimed hundreds of people had landed in hospital across the US as a result of a "clear parasite worm" in Coke's Dasani bottled water.[90] Similarly, telecommunications providers have been bedevilled by fake allegations that 5G wireless technology can damage your health. The COVID-19 pandemic spawned no end of conspiracy theories on vaccines. The list goes on … and on.

TO BE CLEAR...

There's a difference between misinformation, disinformation, and deepfakes. Misinformation is false information spread without a malign motive. By contrast, disinformation has been deliberately fabricated and distributed with the intention of manipulating public opinion or doing harm to a person or institution, including a business. Disinformation often surfaces in the form of rumours and conspiracy theories. A deepfake refers to video, audio, or images that have been expertly altered using AI and other technology to make it seem as if a real person said or did something they didn't actually say or do.

Philip Upton, a partner at PwC and a friend from my time there, noted in a 2021 podcast that while disinformation can wreak damage on any business, some are at higher risk than others:

A celebrity CEO could be targeted by hacks to their social media account. If you're a company that's vocal about its stance on controversial issues, you'll be a target.

If you're a business making a public transactional deal, for example, launching an IPO, rebranding, or reorganizing, you could be a target. If you're a new company experiencing a surge in demand for a particular product or service.

These are a few examples of the type of situation that might cause a disinformation campaign to be launched against you. But it's something that I think pretty much every company needs to be mindful about these days.[91]

The board of the future would be wise to prepare for the dangers and potential costs posed by misinformation, disinformation, and deepfakes. As Holly Gregory, a partner at the US law firm Sidley Austin, wrote in the *Harvard Law School Forum on Corporate Governance*: "Embedding crisis preparedness in board and company culture can help reduce the inevitable tensions that arise when a company is under significant pressure."[92] While the policing of this scourge can—and should—be left in the hands of management, it's the board's responsibility to ensure that plans are in place to respond to fake news about a company's operations. Forceful communication based on careful planning can make all the difference in minimizing this threat.

THE PERILS OF GREENHUSHING

Imagine this: A week before the start of a major international climate conference, an online video surfaces, showing the CEO of a renowned energy firm, hitherto thought to be fully committed to a fast transition to renewable energy, delivering a scathing critique of climate change measures. "The future is coal, it's oil, it's natural gas, and ONLY these reliable energy sources," the authoritative voice declares aggressively. "These climate initiatives? They are nothing but expensive distractions." With a dismissive wave captured in pixel-perfect detail, the clip concludes: "Let's stop this charade of sustainability and focus on the real drivers of our economy and security."

The video goes viral, sending shock waves both through the business community and among environmental activists. But there's a catch. The video is entirely fabricated, a deepfake, a chilling example of artificial intelligence used for malevolent purposes.

The company in question is forced to shift its focus as it scrambles to deal with the bogus message and communicate the truth to the market, employees, and customers. And as everyone is distracted by the deepfake, the company could find itself even more exposed to bad actors in the form of a damaging cyberattack. There's an irony in the situation. The CEO has, over the last year, opted for "greenhushing"—in other words, choosing silence over transparency on environmental issues regarding its environmental initiatives. In doing so, it has inadvertently paved the way for damaging fabrications to take root.

The practice of greenhushing is set to be a contentious topic in the boardroom of the future. Greenhushing and other forms of less-than-open communication are not merely an omission but a gateway to a realm where misinformation and disinformation can thrive unchecked, compromising the trust of stakeholders and the integrity of corporate governance. These practices demand vigilance in the boardroom.

The problem has been exacerbated by the recent backlash against ESG and DEI. While companies continue to pursue their risk-reduction and value-creation work on sustainability, many are not reporting on their progress as openly as they did a few years ago. This void leaves outsiders to draw their own conclusions, however ill-informed. It is also an open invitation to deepfakes to try to tarnish a company's reputation and erode stakeholder trust. The sophistication of deepfake technology has reached a level where hucksters can convincingly fabricate events, making it difficult for stakeholders and the public at large to distinguish between truth and falsehood. While defences against disinformation may be improving, attackers somehow manage to find new ways of evading detection and spreading their fabrications.

In the battle against the underbelly of artificial intelligence, the future board must be vigilant against the perils of misinformation, disinformation, and deepfakes. By implementing proactive communication strategies, investing in detection technology, and fostering a culture of transparency, a board can protect its company and position itself as a paragon of corporate integrity. It is incumbent upon the board not only to oversee robust response plans but to ensure these are ready to deploy at a moment's notice. With such foresight, boards can significantly mitigate the potential damage from digital threats, maintaining stakeholder trust and reinforcing the company's reputation. They can also hope that stakeholders will contact the company and question the validity of the information before passing judgment.

WEIGHING BENEFITS AND RISKS

AI's influence in the boardroom is bound to grow as it takes hold across the business world both as a valuable tool and a serious risk. As such, it will be a critical area for effective governance. Its potential to disrupt long-standing norms underscores the need for both flexibility and continuing vigilance. Likewise, the rapid integration of AI and other advanced technologies, including quantum computing, into almost every facet of business calls for wise direction and well-informed strategies from the boardroom.

Any company wishing to stay competitive in this fast-moving environment will need a board that is not afraid to spearhead bold investments in digital innovation while at the same time demanding the highest ethical standards. In doing so, it will need—as in so many other parts of its work—to be proactive, thinking ahead to seize previously unimagined opportunities and avoid unpleasant surprises. Boards with sufficient resources should consider regular crisis simulations as one way of being prepared for the worst. They also need to keep asking management whether the company is investing enough in the most up-to-date technology and in digitally smart processes. Outside advisers could play a valuable role in this exercise.

Nik Gowing, a former BBC news presenter whose Thinking the Unthinkable project helps leaders understand threats and opportunities in this era of radical uncertainty and disruption, has important advice that applies not only to a board's approach to technology but to every other facet of its work:

I have sympathy with board members who worry about regulation—you have to worry about a whole bundle of things. But in the end, that doesn't mean they should just pick up their coat when they leave the board meeting and say, "Well, I've done my bit for the next two months, I'll come back in two months." This is about every single sensing device being aware that things are changing dramatically and unpredictably far faster than most leaders even start to imagine. If you're in denial about this new and merciless reality of unthinkables, then you have a real problem as a leader. You need to ask: Am I really suited for the job?

A core issue is that conformity is a killer. The conformity which qualifies you to be a leader in so many ways disqualifies you from identifying the scale and nature of disruption, and how to deal with it competently. Indeed, the best thing to do, if you can't cope with this new reality of unthinkables, is to get out and give the job to somebody who's hungry, more aware, and prepared to be more humble and more willing to take risks, including the risk of being fired for taking risks. A good board should be saying to those at the top: "We empower you to take risks to experiment safely, not to fail safely, and we will back you."

One big question is how the boardroom of the future should go about balancing the benefits of advanced technology against the risks and ethical concerns. The answer will seldom be straightforward, but some guidelines can be usefully followed. Most important, AI must never become a vehicle for directors to offload their fiduciary responsibilities. Francesca Ecsery, who serves on the board of Air France, among others, compares a board's use of AI to raising a child:

If the input doesn't go in properly, you get the wrong outcome and you can end up with completely anti-social behaviour. You need to make sure that the input into AI, the algorithms, are good so that you get the right outcomes. You need to test it, you need to parallel-run it for a while, go through a few crises, and see if everybody comes out with the right outcomes. Trust is built over time and we still have a long way to go.

The veteran South African corporate governance expert Mervyn King adds: "You must never forget that you can delegate, but you can't abdicate your responsibility as a director." To put it another way in the context of AI, boards dare not allow machines to make decisions. The big question each board needs to ask is this: Do we as directors, as the collective board, and as a company want to be masters or servants of technology?

In practice, the AI bot should function as a co-pilot to the board, which would limit its use to gathering and analyzing information—in other words, helping to provide the "how" and "what" of boardroom operations. AI's expanding role will recalibrate roles and responsibilities around the boardroom table, covering everything from board composition to decision-making processes. Instead of wrestling with the intricacies of AI, boards should focus on understanding its potential applications and implications. One way to guard against the downsides is to ensure that every new technology is thoroughly tested—for example, by measuring its performance against a twin system in the metaverse, a virtual world where users represented by avatars interact.

Faisal Kazi explains:

What you do is create a digital immersive twin of an actual factory. In other words, you design a factory in the digital world even before the ground is broken in the real world. You can see if the production line is efficient, environmentally friendly, and health-friendly. Once you've optimized the digital space, you can build the factory and have a digital twin of it, a complete replica, and feed it with real-time data. You can solve real-life challenges in the virtual world. You have the ability to do scenario planning, then you can look at the scenarios and balance your financial matrices with sustainability and so on, and make conscious decisions on the physical asset. It's all about simulation, about predicting what will happen. This is where new technologies like machine learning and artificial intelligence come into play. You're doing more and more with less. And you're doing it faster, cheaper, smarter, and safer.

Our future boardroom survey laid out a list of strategies that can help boards smooth the way for unfamiliar new technologies. By far the most popular choice (eight out of ten respondents) was measures to ensure ethical and responsible use of technology, but the replies also included other suggestions that every board would be wise to consider:

- Determining the most relevant aspects of technology innovation for the business and maintaining an open mind about new or emerging technologies

- Understanding the risks and opportunities material to the business

- Acknowledging the economic changes in technology and data

- Encouraging innovation within teams

- Exercising great caution when adopting new technologies

- Clarifying the board's role in setting policies

- Collaborating with professional groups in the field

- Adopting a comprehensive approach that involves all the strategies on the list

Three AI experts at the Chicago-based law firm Mayer Brown pointed out in a September 2023 article in *Directors & Boards* that many companies are updating their policies to address concerns about potential risks and harms in the context of generative AI, such as bias and discrimination, confidentiality, consumer protection, cybersecurity, data security, privacy, quality control, and trade secrets.[93] Every board should ensure that its organization is following suit.

As in other areas of governance, education will be a vital component in equipping the boardroom of the future with the means to understand and navigate the risks and rewards of evolving technology. Indeed, more than two-thirds of respondents to our future boardroom survey foresee an increased focus on digital literacy training for directors. That finding is reinforced by PensionDanmark's former chief executive Torben Möger Pedersen, who recommends that instead of recruiting a single AI expert to the board, every director should have some expertise in this area: "All board members have to train themselves to have a basic understanding at least of the possibilities of AI in their industry because that will become a fundamental part of the way products and processes are designed in all kinds of industries."

Whatever form that training takes, it must nurture an awareness among board members that AI can never be a substitute for human interaction. "You really don't want to lose the human element," says Eric Wetlaufer, a director of Canada's TMX Group and the Investment Management Corporation of Ontario. "AI has to be complemented by engagement with the company. Some of the best insights I get are not from meeting with the CEO and his or her team, but with the salespeople or the risk people in between the board meetings." Or, as Nasdaq's Byron Loflin puts it: "Being a great board member is being the best human you can be, bringing your full self into the boardroom and being active."

SOME PRACTICAL ADVICE

As I emphasized earlier, AI and other advanced technologies do not alter the fundamental fiduciary duties of a director. Board members must continue to act in the best interests of the corporation.

AN AI CHECKLIST FOR THE BOARDROOM OF THE FUTURE

Reggie Townsend, who leads SAS's data ethics practice, has a list of questions that board members should be asking their executive team about AI and technology in general:

How does AI impact our mission? Do we need to reconsider the direction of the organization as a consequence of this new technology? To what degree?

How are we potentially impacted by this technology? Are we a provider of it or are we just a consumer? Do we have the right people in place to properly provide or consume it?

Are we in a position to properly operationalize this technology such that we stay clear of potential regulatory concerns?

What are the regulatory concerns? What does the regulatory environment look like today? What might it look like in five to ten years?

What data do we need? How long do we need it? How are we going to dispose of it eventually?

How are we using this data, and how are we protecting it? To what degree will we store this data? When will this data no longer be important for the decisions we need to make?

When it comes to specific countermeasures, the board's role should be both protective and strategic. Corporate leaders must recognize the gravity of digital threats and take decisive action. Here are some measures for the board of the future to consider:

- **Establish a robust communication protocol.** In the event of a deepfake crisis, a well-prepared plan with rapid response capabilities can prevent the escalation of disinformation and protect the company's reputation.

- **Invest in detection technology.** Boards should advocate for investment in sophisticated technology capable of detecting deepfakes and other forms of synthetic media, enabling the company to identify and address fraudulent content quickly.

- **Educate and train.** Implement comprehensive training for senior managers and board members to recognize and understand the impact of false information and deepfakes. An informed workforce can act as the first defence against the spread of manipulated information.

- **Enhance transparency.** Promote regular, detailed disclosures about company practices and policies. Transparency not only builds trust with stakeholders but also serves as a deterrent against those who might seek to damage the company.

- **Engage stakeholders.** Cultivate a dialogue with stakeholders to reinforce the company's commitment to authenticity and truth. Stakeholder engagement can also provide a supportive network to counteract the spread of disinformation.

- **Develop strategic partnerships.** Collaborate with other businesses, industry groups, and regulatory bodies to set standards and best practices for combatting misinformation and deepfakes.

- **Pursue legal and regulatory advocacy.** Take an active role in advocating for more effective regulations and laws to counter the creation and dissemination of deepfakes and similar abuses, thus helping to establish a legal framework that deters such activities.

- **Decide if "greenhushing" is the right strategy.** Make time for a discussion and decide the pros and cons of not being open about the progress the company is making.

- **Foster proactive communication.** Make key stakeholders aware of the views of the board and leadership on sustainability and climate matters, and the reasons for opting for "greenhushing," or not.

- **Appoint a commander in charge.** A dedicated person can ensure transparent and consistent communication regarding the company's sustainability efforts. He or she can communicate regularly to the board, work on mitigating the risks of greenhushing, and provide a credible source of information. This will often require material data to be verified by a trusted third party.

More broadly, every director should be asking: Am I prepared to welcome the changes driven by AI and other advanced technologies? How do I plan to navigate this evolving landscape? How will I ensure that I have the insight needed to provide the oversight that directors are obligated to exercise? The answers to these questions will determine how well equipped you and your board are to meet the demands of the AI era.

///

Ten Questions for the Board of the Future

1. In what ways is your board integrating AI into its decision-making processes and meeting preparations?

2. Can you name three potential benefits that AI could bring to your company over the next year and the next decade?

3. Can you name three threats that AI could pose to your company?

4. Can you name three ethical issues that your board will need to grapple with in relation to AI and other advanced technologies?

5. What training, if any, have you and your fellow board members had in AI and other advanced technologies?

6. How is your board staying informed about the latest advancements in AI and other emerging technologies?

7. What measures has your company implemented to enhance cyber-resilience, and how is the board involved in overseeing these measures?

8. Has your company been a victim of a cyberattack? If so, what action did the board take? Is cyber resilience prioritized?

9. What policies are in place to prepare for and respond to a cyberattack or to disinformation or deepfakes that affect your company?

10. What oversight mechanism(s) has your board put in place to fulfill its fiduciary duties on the implementation of advanced technology?

CHAPTER EIGHT

From Shareholders to Stakeholders

Always make decisions in the best long-term interests of the company, because if the board as a collective mind gets that right, it's in the best long-term interests of all stakeholders. But if you focus just on one stakeholder, for example, the shareholder, then you're not going to get that right.

—*Mervyn King, chair emeritus, King Code of Corporate Governance, South Africa*

In her role as a director of several well-known multinational companies, Claudia Sender Ramirez makes a point of casting a wide net to assess what others think of the job she and her fellow directors are doing. She does this in three ways:

First, I try to listen to customers. When it's a company that has stores, I try to visit a store to see what customers are talking about and read the customer reports that we get from the operations. Second, I try to interact with younger employees because, in general, they're so much more in tune with what is happening. There's this concept of shadow boards, where you bring younger employees to talk to the board members and have a discussion, which I think is very healthy. These people are in general closer to the customer so they have a better sense of the upcoming things that the board will have to deal with in the future. And third, I try to understand what is being said about the company not only inside the company but outside, because otherwise you get too much of what I call a belly-button view. What I'm trying to do as a board member is gather external information, bring it inside, and think about how we want to adapt.

The boardroom of the future will need many more directors like Sender Ramirez. The importance of active, wide-ranging stakeholder engagement comes through loud and clear in the Competent Boards future boardroom survey. No fewer than 80 percent of respondents say that active involvement in environmental and social issues will be critical for board members. Almost as many take the view that rising stakeholder expectations for transparency, accountability, and social and environmental impact will pose a major challenge for the board of the future. Given these views, it is no wonder that more than three-quarters of respondents cite "proactive shareholder engagement" as a critical way for boards to stay informed and responsive. About 12 percent single out "active engagement with a diverse set of stakeholders" as one way in which a board should be keeping abreast of its sustainability and social responsibilities.

Several respondents point to the importance of understanding geopolitical and macroeconomic trends and adapting to them. Likewise, they anticipate that boards will become more involved in governance and oversight issues and less in performance and operations, with a premium on foresight—in other words, anticipating the future. All this requires knowledge which is difficult, if not impossible, to acquire without reaching out to experts at think-tanks, trade associations, non-governmental organizations, political parties, and many more. Indeed, 77 percent of our survey's respondents recommend that the board of the future should make greater use of external advisers and experts as a way of encouraging adaptability and forward thinking.

On the flip side, the survey suggests that stakeholder and governance issues are among the thorniest that board members face in integrating environmental, social, and governance factors into their decision-making. Those issues include shareholder buy-in, rising stakeholder activism, and legal constraints related to stakeholder rights. Respondents acknowledge that short-term, profit-driven shareholders spark tensions in the boardroom, especially when their goals conflict with long-term sustainability efforts.

THE ACTIVISTS ARE COMING

Gone are the days when board members were considered to be in touch with a company's affairs if they showed up for quarterly management presentations and the annual meeting. The mere fact that the word "shareholders" has made way for "stakeholders" in so many contexts is evidence of the realization that boards are responsible to a much wider group of constituents than in the past. Reaching out beyond the company, as Sender Ramirez does, means talking not only to investors but also to customers, suppliers, bankers, regulators, local community leaders, and more. Even activists—especially those who are less friendly than the company may wish—can be valuable sounding boards, providing useful information and opinions that board members may not hear from anyone else.

Given that no business can ever entirely separate itself from the society and environment where it operates, the necessity for board members to reach out to the widest possible group of stakeholders is only likely to grow, making it one of the flagship themes of this book.

The benefits of a board casting its net as widely as possible are incalculable. The more outside parties a board takes an interest in, the better the chances of it getting ahead of its rivals and nipping trouble in the bud. Companies that are plugged into the world around them are more likely to spot emerging trends in consumer behaviour, product innovation, marketing strategies, and government regulation, to name just a few, making them better equipped to be leaders rather than followers. Boards of consumer-oriented companies, such as retailers, clothing manufacturers, and utilities, have an extra incentive to stay in touch with outside stakeholders. Those who pay the most attention to what consumers are telling them are also the most likely to stay ahead of their rivals and, as a result, will be best placed to charge premium prices on their products. For every company, in whatever sector, the value of staying ahead of the pack cannot be overstated at a time when the regulatory landscape on so many issues is shifting fast, filled with uncertainty and varying widely from one part of the world to another.

Conversely, the cost to boards that fail to keep their ears to the ground is also mounting. Investors who might have walked away in the past from a company that was not performing to expectations are now more inclined to stick around and push for change. Using a strategy known as impact investment or active engagement, they are more likely to press their case with board members and senior management, often on behalf of advocacy groups, local communities, and others affected by the company's operations.

The Danish pension fund PensionDanmark, for example, boasts that its policy of "active ownership" not only expands its investment opportunities, but reinforces its ability to help solve some of the big issues facing society.[94] "In most companies, an active engagement with their owners is a value-creating process if they're doing it in the right way," says PensionDanmark's former chief executive Torben Möger Pedersen. "Our experience is that many companies have a very positive reaction to this. The underlying trend is that dialogue between companies and shareholders is much more alive than at any time before."

Another emerging concept that should be on every board's radar is "additionality"—in other words, using capital to tackle society's challenges in new ways or tackling problems that are not currently being addressed.[95] Recent regulatory measures, such as the Sustainability Disclosure Requirements published by the UK's Financial Conduct Authority, underscore the importance of articulating an investment as a "solution provider" as a way of ensuring the accuracy of sustainability-related terms and preventing greenwashing.[96]

Boards that cling to the notion that their responsibility is confined to maximizing shareholder value should be prepared for stiff pushback. In one such—ultimately unsuccessful—example, the environmental law firm ClientEarth brought a lawsuit in the UK in 2023 against all eleven directors of Royal Dutch Shell, one of the world's largest oil and gas producers.[97] ClientEarth contended that, notwithstanding record annual profits, the oil major's directors had mismanaged climate risk and breached their duty because Shell's climate transition strategy could not achieve its target of net-zero carbon emissions by 2050. Much of ClientEarth's case was based on a 2006 reform of the UK Companies Act that added a new provision for actions by shareholders, including, for the first time, a specific reference to the environment. In dismissing the case, the judge found that ClientEarth's witnesses were not sufficiently expert in the field, that it had not brought the case in good faith, and that there was no universally accepted method as to how Shell might be able to achieve its energy transition targets.[98] While ClientEarth may not have prevailed in this case, its lawsuit illustrates the growing activism that the board of the future will face. As one British lawyer told *The Guardian*, "The further expansion of the discussion around how the courts will assess similar claims will be helpful to future activists considering how to bring claims involving directors' duties and boards' approach to climate change with a better chance of success."[99]

SOME WAYS TO REACH OUT

As long ago as 1998, when the word "stakeholder" barely existed, the International Finance Corporation, a division of the World Bank, published a "good practice manual" for effective public consultation and disclosure. Its advice is as relevant to the boardroom of the future as it was a quarter of a century ago. "Good public consultation costs money," the report noted, "but poor public consultation can cost a lot more."[100]

While it makes little sense for a board to have representatives from each and every stakeholder group around the table, directors need to find ways of tapping into the views, no matter how uncomfortable, of those with a tangible interest in the business. After all, as I pointed out in *Stewards of the Future*, feedback on company policies and practices is far more valuable before they are implemented than having to deal with unhappy customers, suppliers, employees, or neighbours.

The first step in such a proactive process should be a discussion to identify critical stakeholders and determine which directors are best equipped to make contact with each of them. Next, set up a transparent process for communication with these groups along similar lines to the investor and analyst meetings that are already a fixture on most boards' agendas. Directors also need to consider how best to tap into the knowledge and opinions of other groups that may be less important to the company but may still have a valuable contribution to make. I believe that board members should meet regularly with current and potential stakeholders, and report on these relationships. One way of doing this is to set up an advisory panel of stakeholders, perhaps more than one.

The format of stakeholder meetings should take account of the participants' culture and customs. Some may be more informal than others. Some may be smaller than others. Some may be held in the boardroom, others at more remote locations. And so on. The key point is that directors can fulfill their fiduciary duty only if they have the knowledge and the approach needed to ask the right questions and to interpret the answers in a way that best serves the company's short- and long-term interests.

THE NOVO NORDISK WAY

The Danish pharmaceuticals maker Novo Nordisk, best known for its diabetes drugs Ozempic and Rybelsus, has shown what genuine stakeholder engagement looks like.

Just six months after Lars Rebien Sørensen took the reins of the company in 2001, a group of activists gathered in front of one of its plants to protest a decision by Novo Nordisk and forty other drugmakers to sue the South African government over patent rights for drugs used to treat HIV/AIDS. Far from calling the police or sheltering in his office, Sørensen took off his tie, put on a leather jacket, and walked out to meet the protesters.

"I'm now in a place where I have to make everything come together in the sense that, of course we have to make money, but we have to do it in the right way, so we can look at ourselves in the mirror," Sørensen told *MedWatch*, a Danish trade journal, in 2014. "You have to create a coherent corporate story. Call it what you want, but simply put, it's a matter of describing clearly what the company stands for and where the company is trying to get to. It has to be described in a way so that employees, potential employees, and stakeholders outside the company can all identify with it and identify the company with it.

"There is an old native-American saying that describes it quite well: 'If you want to travel quickly, travel alone. If you want to travel far, travel together.'

We don't want to be too quick, we want to be sustainable in the long run. If the company has a strong profile and a strong history, it will attract the people that such a profile and history resonates with."

Boards today face a whirlwind of technological advancements and societal expectations, where information travels at the speed of a tweet and crises can escalate in mere minutes. In this high-stakes environment, a passive board is a liability. The board of the future will only thrive if it evolves from a gatekeeper to a deeply engaged architect of long-term resilience.

Stakeholder satisfaction is no longer a "nice to have"—it's a survival strategy. Investors may have dictated the narrative in the past, but tomorrow's success hinges equally on understanding the pulse of employees, communities, and partners. A disgruntled supplier or an ignored societal issue can quickly snowball into reputational and financial disaster.

Consider the fallout from misaligned partnerships or affiliations. Public backlash against companies with ties to unethical suppliers or groups perceived as misaligned with societal values has eroded market positions overnight. A recent example involved Shein, the fast-fashion retailer. In June 2024, reports surfaced alleging that Shein's supply chain lacked transparency, particularly concerning the use of cotton sourced from China's Xinjiang region, an area associated with forced labour practices involving the local Uyghur population. These allegations intensified scrutiny from US regulators and politicians, especially as Shein was pursuing an initial public offering of its shares in the US. The company's perceived lack of transparency and potential ties to unethical labour practices sparked a public backlash, raising concerns about its supply chain integrity and corporate responsibility.[101]

This means due diligence cannot remain a box-ticking exercise—it must be rigorous, real-time, and predictive. The same applies to Mergers & Acquisitions: vetting prospective buyers or sellers isn't just about the bottom line but about the ethical and reputational ripple effects of those deals.

Boards must also adopt a "radar and response" model. This requires investing in tech tools that provide real-time insights into stakeholder sentiment, supply chain integrity, and value alignment. It also means engaging more frequently and directly with stakeholder groups rather than relying solely on filtered reports.

Failure to engage fully—and equitably—across these domains won't just dent the share price; it will obliterate the licence to operate in an increasingly unforgiving public and regulatory landscape.

The Competent Boards network members has other thought-provoking words of advice on how the board of the future can reach out to its various constituencies.

R. Gopalakrishnan says that during his time on various Tata boards, he learned to ask three questions before taking any decision: "First, is it good for my nation or community or whatever you want to call it? Second, is it good for my employees and my partners? And third, is it good for my shareholders?" All too often these questions are asked in the opposite order: first shareholders, then employees, then community. But in Gopalakrishnan's experience, inverting the pyramid tends to produce far wiser decisions.

He also learned to appreciate the benefits of interacting with social and environmental activists. "When I'm a director, I tend to think of an activist as being like a fly," Gopalakrishnan says. "He's a bit of a nuisance, he's buzzing around my ear, and I wish I could just sort that person out and get on with my work. But unless you learn to deal with this fly with respect, it will bother you. As Anita Roddick, the founder of Body Shop, said: 'If you think you're too small to have an impact, try going to bed with a mosquito in the room.' You know, that activist is not going to go away."

HOW KINDER MORGAN LISTENED TO ONE COMMUNITY

As You Sow, a non-profit shareholder representative organization, set up a "racial justice initiative" in June 2020 following George Floyd's murder. One of the team's early initiatives was to work with US pipeline operator Kinder Morgan to address toxic emissions from a plant that had been polluting the Dutchtown community on the banks of the Mississippi River near St. Louis for years. Andrew Behar, As You Sow's CEO, describes what happened:

> The citizens there had been complaining, but the company never listened to them. We're talking about elementary schools, hospitals, and elder care facilities downwind from the facility. We sat down with the community, listened to them, and brought what they had been saying

to the company in the form of a shareholder resolution. They escalated it to the board that didn't even know. We presented the risk factors, saying, "This is really bad for the brand and therefore is a material risk to the company, as it's going to affect us as shareholders and we want this addressed." That is the core of what a shareholder's legal rights are.

That led to several meetings with the community. They brought in the mayor, the local member of Congress, and a state senator. They also brought in other local emitters because Kinder Morgan wasn't the only one. Now, they're actually creating a better situation. They've just finished helping the community build new parks and schools. Throughout 2022, Kinder Morgan provided quarterly progress check-ins to the racial justice team.

We helped the company gain access to decision-makers to find mutually beneficial solutions. That's what we do, that is our theory of change. If we don't find it immediately, we don't give up. We back up and try another path. We are incredibly tenacious.

We want to know our products are good, and they're safe. That provides clarity for our employees and for our customers. The better boards of directors are saying, "We want good governance on the board level so you don't need as much regulation. Self-governance leads to a market advantage."

For Eric Wetlaufer, a director of Canada's TMX Group and the Investment Management Corporation of Ontario, open-mindedness and initiative are key to dealing with stakeholders:

Boards need to be adaptive. They need to be able to anticipate and respond more quickly to changes in the environment. They need to think more about scenarios and risks that the company faces as well as opportunities. They need to think more openly about partnering with other companies and with other institutions, whether it be governments or whatever. They can't be so closed-minded that they think they have to invent everything, do everything themselves, and protect everything. They have to be attractive for customers, employees, stakeholders, and partners to work with. Just because you're big doesn't mean you're going to win. To thrive, you must appeal to all your stakeholders, inspiring them to invest their time and resources with you. As the choices available to individuals and businesses continue to expand, standing out has never been more critical.

One of the most important things that people don't talk about and people don't do much of is to curate your own stakeholders. Don't accept that the people who are around the board table are the people that you have to have around the board table. Don't accept that the current shareholders of your company are going to forever be the future shareholders. Don't accept that the current customers are going to be the future customers. You have the opportunity to curate those people and those organizations that you work with and that you depend on. If you don't like it, if it's not working for you, go out and change it. Do the work to put the people in place that are going to create a more resilient, more successful firm in the long term. That's up to you.

South Africa's Mervyn King emphasizes the importance of compromise:

The board has to focus on the inside-out impact on the economy, society, and the environment. The activities inside the company in making its product result in impacts on those three critical dimensions for sustainable development. Also one must accept that sustainability, like a coin, has two sides so those three dimensions also impact from the outside in on a company. For example, the collapse of Lehman Brothers and the global financial crisis had a huge impact on companies' balance sheets and operational performance.

On the boards that I chaired we created a new corporate animal, the corporate stakeholder relationship officer. Part of the job description was that he or she had to have been a chief executive of a limited liability company. The person the board appointed in one particular company took about eighteen months to get everyone to understand the purpose of the company's business. The board understood the stakeholders' needs, interests, and expectations but always took a decision in the best long-term interests of the health of the company. A board, for example, has to understand how its suppliers are being governed. If a supplier is breaching human rights and this becomes publicly known, a consumer company could suffer up to a 50 percent loss in its market cap on the next day of trading.

Communication is also key for Yasuhiro Kawasugi, who has held various positions at Konica Minolta in Europe, the UK, and Japan:

> We usually have a one-hour engagement meeting with institutional investors which we can use efficiently and effectively. For example, in recent meetings they asked to review three policies of the board for this fiscal year and the progress on executive capability mentioned by the chairman in our integrated report.
>
> It's very helpful for us to have the engagement meeting. We can start a deeper discussion based on investors' understanding of our company and their thoughts on material issues, including sustainability issues. Our integrated report doesn't just describe the superficial form of the company but has messages from board members, including outside directors, and executive members and even, for example, employees and customers who provide a timely and lively voice.
>
> What I've learned is that investors carefully read the integrated report. It's a very good tool for communication. Of course, we change the content of the communication for different investors, such as short-term investors or any individual investors. We tend to pursue long-term investors, so communication based on the integrated report is very helpful to have.

For the Aspen Institute's Erika Karp, the secret of effective stakeholder engagement is directors who keep their ears and eyes open, and then ask the right questions:

You need to understand the potential risks that come up in certain sectors. For example, human trafficking is a real issue for airlines and restaurants and hotels; sexual and gender-based violence for technology companies and the media. As a board director, you know that those issues are out there. So let's understand them, let's study what's going on, what might be going on in our company, and then let's make sure that we have processes in place to identify and hold accountable those who are opening up the company to risk. It's a matter of educating ourselves as board members, not turning a blind eye, not being complicit based on ignorance, or just not knowing that it's not okay.

Andrew Behar goes even further, suggesting that the board of the future should look for ways of institutionalizing stakeholder engagement:

All those different stakeholders should have a voice in the boardroom. Either a board seat or, at minimum, on an advisory committee. Imagine if all stakeholders were represented: a community advisory committee, an employee advisory committee. Some companies are holding a seat for a person to represent nature, with enough power so that the board needs to listen to them. They're going to give you the diversity of thought needed to find ways to solve problems before it becomes a problem. We all need to be aware of it and need to have metrics to measure it. My recommendation is that each stakeholder group should be listened to and should have a mechanism by which they can raise issues. Situational awareness for the board is critical.

THE BENEFITS ARE WORTH THE EFFORT

Paul Polman, who spearheaded the revival of the Anglo-Dutch consumer products giant Unilever, summed up the benefits of engaging with a wide range of stakeholders in a 2021 *Harvard Business Review* article co-authored with sustainable business strategy expert Andrew Winston:

> Net-positive companies build better connections with stakeholders besides employees … They forge bonds with suppliers by helping to grow and improve their businesses, rather than simply demanding the lowest cost … They also help consumers lead more sustainable lives, support business customers on their sustainability journey, and find and work with investors who want long-term value creation. And, in turn, communities with stronger ties to an organization support it through good times and bad.
>
> Having a wide array of stakeholders, bound by purpose and all trusting and working in partnership with the company, provides a diverse bank of support. Remember those palm trees surviving big storms? Part of their secret is a large, spread-out root system—not just one anchor but many that can take a lot of pressure.[102]

The relevance of these observations extends far beyond palm trees. The founder of India's Tata group and the father of modern Indian industry, Jamsetji Tata, noted more than a century ago: "In a free enterprise, the community is not just another stakeholder in business, but is in fact the very purpose of its existence."

As board members ponder their duty to engage beyond the narrow confines of the company they serve, Mervyn King's wise words are also worth bearing in mind: "The company that you and I are directors of is not on an island. It's part of the globe. Success does not just mean making an increased profit, but means you have actually added value to society in the long term."

III

Ten Questions for the Board of the Future

1. How does your board prioritize and balance the needs of various stakeholders (for example, shareholders, employees, customers, suppliers, communities, and regulators)?

2. What proactive measures does your board take to engage with investors beyond routine meetings and reports?

3. How does your board ensure transparency and alignment with suppliers?

4. In what ways does your board solicit and act on customer, supplier, employee, and other stakeholder feedback?

5. What mechanisms are in place for your board to engage with employees across all levels, especially to gain insights into workplace culture and emerging challenges?

6. How does your board collaborate with regulators and government officials to navigate changing laws and policies, ensuring both compliance and strategic foresight?

7. What role does your board play in building relationships with advocacy groups, and how does it incorporate their feedback into governance and strategy?

8. How does your board stay informed about local community needs and concerns, and how are these insights integrated into the company's long-term plans?

9. How often does your board convene in different locations to gain first-hand insights, and how does this practice inform your decisions?

10. Is stakeholder engagement a formal, recurring agenda item in your board meetings? If so, how does the board measure and review the effectiveness of these engagements?

CHAPTER NINE

The Wise Chair

When you're chair of the board, it's not just about what you ask and how clever you are. It's about getting the cleverness out of other people.

—R. Gopalakrishnan, former executive director of Tata Sons

I wish I could say that board chairs of the future will have an easier job than their predecessors. After all, they will have access to a once-unimaginable range of expertise and technology. The domineering personalities who typically led corporate boards in the past are gradually making way for kinder, gentler types with stronger people skills. And the drive for improved governance is nudging companies to separate the roles of chair and chief executive, enabling the chair to focus on the big picture rather than being caught up in operational minutiae. If nothing else were changing in the boardroom, the chair of the future would surely have more time for consultation, reflection, and calm leadership.

In reality, however, the person at the head of the table will have an even heavier burden on their shoulders. Every

Competent Boards network member agrees that no job on a board has more potential than the chair to create or destroy value. Yet far from being simpler, the chair's job is becoming more complex and more demanding. For a start, companies—and their boards—are under more intense scrutiny than in the past. Led by the chair, boards will have to pay more attention to topics that, until recently, seemed to have no place on a board agenda. It has become increasingly difficult—and unwise—to ignore the threats posed by pandemics, far-off conflicts, climate change, geopolitics, biodiversity, artificial intelligence, cybersecurity, and tougher disclosure requirements, among others. These issues are forcing chairs and their boards to spend more time on matters such as social responsibility, supply-chain problems, employee well-being, social media, and, not least, sustainability (however one may choose to define that).

A DIFFERENT LEADERSHIP STYLE

Even the way meetings are run these days calls for a new kind of leadership in the boardroom. The growing emphasis on a diversity of ideas and a variety of cultural insights puts a premium on compromise and consensus. In this digital era, the dynamics, not to mention the technology, of a virtual get-together can be quite different from an in-person gathering.

The chair of the future will encourage a diversity of views accompanied by a spirit of compromise around the board-room table. That may involve inviting more outside experts to board meetings and setting up advisory committees that may include members of senior management. It certainly involves the chair (and other board members) asking questions rather than pontificating on their own experience and parlaying their own supposed words of wisdom. Shailesh Haribhakti, who has led more than a dozen Indian companies, calls this the "team board" approach. "The board should not consist of opinionated people who just want to make sure that what they think or say goes," Haribhakti says. "The chairperson should build consensus around what ought to be done to secure a fantastic future for the company."

South African corporate governance expert Mervyn King says, only half-jokingly, that "people think that to be chair is honorific. I say it's horrific." He explains:

> Sometimes you've got to deal with horrible situations. And as the chair, you have to make decisions, and you've got to be seen to be acting responsibly, and to help the company be seen as a responsible corporate citizen. You've got to have a stature because the expectation is that the chairman is responsible for everything. If ever there was an expectation gap, there it is. The man in the street says: "Whoa, that's the chair. You see what happened to that company?" So that's why I say to be the chair is actually horrific.

The Competent Boards network members have some words of advice for those who aspire to chair the board of tomorrow:

- Be sure to have an interest and expertise in sustainability issues like human rights, climate change, and nature. Without such competencies, the chair will struggle to meet stakeholders' growing expectation that these issues will be integrated into the company's strategy and operations.

- Be ready to navigate complex geopolitical issues that affect global operations and supply chains. That means paying attention to diverse perspectives on potential risks.

- Keep abreast of advances in technology, given the enormously disruptive influence of AI and other innovations. The chair should also make sure that other board members understand the implications of these technologies for their company.

- Take a long-term, multi-stakeholder approach to governance, ensuring that the board becomes ever more accountable not only to shareholders but to others with an interest in the company's well-being.

- Never lose sight of due diligence and accountability across the entire spectrum of the company's operations. That includes close scrutiny of supply chains for human-rights abuses and environmental impact, as well as keeping track of any damage caused by sold products, such as plastic bags or bottles, and the treatment of disused production sites.

A CRUCIAL, SOMETIMES UNCOMFORTABLE RELATIONSHIP

No board can function effectively without a strong working relationship between the chair and the chief executive. They don't have to like each other (though that certainly helps), but they do have to respect each other, communicate with each other, and listen to each other. Michael Treschow, past chairman of Unilever, Ericsson, and the Confederation of Swedish Enterprise, sees one of the chair's main jobs in the future as being a coach to the CEO and "making sure you understand [each other] and work well together." Treschow believes that the chair has two other key responsibilities: first, making sure that the board agenda is geared towards strategy rather than operational issues; and second, encouraging board members to express a variety of views and then making sure that the board as a whole takes the necessary decisions and gets through its agenda.

Experience as a CEO may help in taking on the mantle of a chair, but it also carries risks. Sarah Kaplan, of the Rotman School of Management at the University of Toronto, notes a crucial difference between the two roles: the CEO tends to be a "content" person while the chair typically focuses on process. The board of the future, Kaplan advises, would be unwise to appoint a present or former CEO as its chair:

> The roles are diametrically opposed. When you have been in management and then you get on a board, it's really hard to keep your fingers out because you have been "fingers-in" as a leader. You have been running things, you have been charged with knowing and directing things. And then when you get on a board, your job is to ask the hard questions. Of course, there are times when boards make decisions, but most of the value that comes from a board is stress-testing management. When you're the chair, you're meant to be enabling the conversation, not voicing your opinion. You have to switch your mindset, and that's a massive switch.

For many years the assumption was that a board chair would look and act much like a chief executive and come from a similar background. But that is likely to be less so in the future. As New York University's Tensie Whelan notes:

> Because times are changing so rapidly, the people who were running companies ten or fifteen years ago don't necessarily have the right skills and understanding to be as helpful to the current CEOs as maybe was the case thirty to forty years ago.
>
> CEOs would benefit more from having people who will help them think outside of the box, rather than helping them think within a box that they knew fifteen years ago. That's not to say there aren't CEOs who've stepped down and who keep up and think of new things, but we need to identify board chairs who bring in more expansive thinking, who are versed in stakeholder capitalism and not only shareholder capitalism, who understand that nobody can be an expert in everything but believe in the need to focus on a key set of issues.

Another weakness of many existing boards is the obsequious deference that directors show to the company's chief executive. For whatever reason, directors prefer not to upset the applecart by questioning the actions of a powerful CEO. Some may be wary of disrupting their social networks; some may fear losing the prestige or remuneration that comes with a board appointment; and others may simply prefer to "go with the flow." That attitude will need to change on the board of the future.

Peter Dey, a former Ontario Securities Commission chair who has gained a reputation as the godfather of Canadian governance, believes that the chair should play the key role in defining and developing the culture of the corporation and in setting the board agenda. Artificial intelligence is a good example. "This is an issue the corporation should fully understand, and the board chair should ensure management is applying the proper resources to determining the impact of AI on the corporation."

Chairs can also assert the board's authority by spearheading the drive for greater diversity in the boardroom. As discussed in chapter six, people from different social and business backgrounds are less likely to adopt a herd mentality or fear the consequences of speaking their mind. The chair is a critical catalyst in encouraging such a culture. As Sarah Kaplan puts it:

> Boardroom conversations are going to have to be much more uncomfortable. Every single person has the obligation to speak up, and the board chair has the obligation to make sure everyone speaks up, especially those who tend to be quiet or those whose views tend to be neglected. There's a lot more onus on the board chair to be a good process manager, to be a good facilitator, to be good in engaging around the uncomfortable moments. Chairs need to guide the conversation to points of tension, because that's really where all the action is.

SETTING THE AGENDA

The chair of the future will be more active than their predecessors in shaping the board agenda towards the big issues that face the business down the road. Today, the agenda is all too often a standardized list of accounts and reports with the most interesting and consequential issues squeezed in at the end. The board of the future will put greater emphasis on risk, oversight, fiduciary obligations, and long-term strategy. Veteran director Francesca Ecsery elaborates:

> The best meetings are when the chairperson is well prepared, has had several conversations with the executives, understands what the key issues are, and then sends a quick e-mail to the rest of the board saying "You've got the papers, you've read them all. Out of the papers and out of my conversations, these are the three things we need to spend time on. Once we've done that, we can go into the standard items." Then you spend the time debating the quality items that are most useful for the business.

Ecsery has some thoughts on how the future board can move in that direction:

> You need good board papers. I sometimes get six hundred pages and I wonder how on earth I'm supposed to find out what the key priorities are. Somebody needs to distill this. Some businesses are more complex than others, so you need to spend more time on the detail. You need to have additional discussions with the executives. You need to have really good questions because you can't tell people what to do. You have to get them to do it.

A TIME FOR TACT, A TIME FOR RUTHLESSNESS

Karen Loon, a member of the INSEAD Directors Network, made the astute observation in a 2021 article that being a chair is not about possessing one attribute or another, but rather combining opposite pairs of attributes.[103] Loon singled out five such pairs:

- Authority and humility
- Commitment and detachment
- Incisiveness and patience
- Helicopter view and company knowledge
- Hard and soft skills

Some of these characteristics are likely to take on special importance in coming years. Thus, a helicopter view (in other words, keeping your eyes firmly on the big picture) will certainly play a bigger role than it used to. Cultivating a broad outlook, according to R. Gopalakrishnan, enables chairs to ask questions that may not have occurred to other directors or even the chief executive. For example: What is the role of this company in society? What are the good principles that it should be following? Where is the potential to improve?

Peter Dey says that a chair must instill a chemistry on the board that encourages all directors to air their various perspectives. At the same time, the chair should have the skill to move a discussion to a consensus or, when a consensus is not possible, to move on. Two other attributes worth adding to Loon's list are tact and ruthlessness. Drawing on his own experience, Mervyn King recalls a couple of occasions when he used each of them:

> I was chairman of a merchant bank and a director of its retail business. We built a new head office in a major city and I had a beautiful office … Persian carpets, marble floor.

But it was discovered that the sole shareholder of the interior decorator was the chief executive's daughter, which was not disclosed. There certainly was an inquiry. And needless to say, the chief executive left the company. That inquiry was one of the most uncomfortable things I've ever done in my life, but I had to do it. Why?

I'd been to his house for dinner, he'd been to my house for dinner. His wife and my wife played bridge together. We'd been to social functions for the bank together. What did I learn? As the chair, you've got to be collegial, but at the same time, you've got to be at arm's length with your fellow directors.

If you look around the world, a director's duties are good faith, care, skill, and diligence. People keep forgetting the diligence. That means when you get that thirty-page management pack, you should diligently go through it, understand it, and then make a meaningful contribution to a discussion before the board as a collective mind makes a business judgment call on behalf of the company.

As chair, I used to do the following: I would phone a non-executive director because I thought he or she had some knowledge about a certain aspect. I would ask: "Have you read your board pack?" Then I would say: "I want you to go into greater detail. Wikipedia, Google … do what you like but I will ask you to start the discussion, and I want you to add more than is in the management report from your research."

At the meeting we'd have a forty-five-minute discussion and I would say that I can see the board is inclined to decision ABC. Do you agree with that? I would then just pick on one director and say, "Jack, can you please explain to me in detail why you voted yes?" Now if Jack hasn't understood this thirty-page management report, the additional directors' report, the forty-five-minute discussion, has been present but not observing or understanding or has not done his homework and been diligent, he is going to sit there with two rows of teeth in his mouth.

From that time, I would know that my board members had done their homework, because they knew I was going to do that. I didn't do it at every board meeting. Also, no one spoke across the table about something, but everybody spoke through me. And that's how one controls a board.

Small gestures and informal rituals can often make the difference between a skillful chair and a mediocre one. In order to avoid conflict around the boardroom table, for example, a wise chair can encourage breakout sessions where directors discuss a contentious matter among themselves or with management, and then report back to the chair. "There are many tricks," says Michael Treschow. "The chair needs to make sure that everybody is not sitting there flipping with airline tickets, or whatever. When the room becomes deadly silent and we all look at one person, it won't happen again. It can seem like nothing has changed since we were in the classroom!"

TRUST AND TRUTH ARE ESSENTIAL

Whether exercising authority or humility, tact or ruthlessness, hard or soft skills, a chair has few more fundamental tasks than to engender trust and be faithful to the truth. A business cannot survive without trust among board members, between board members and senior executives, and between the company and its stakeholders. And building trust is well-nigh impossible if all these players are not being honest with each other. That is especially important in a polarized world marked by a never-ending avalanche of fake news. Others can choose to agree or disagree with the chosen course, but it is up to the board—and especially the chair—to ensure that leadership is talking with one voice and that its pronouncements are consistent with the facts.

Gopalakrishnan recalls how he sought to engender mutual trust and respect during his time in the chair at various Tata subsidiaries:

> I said there's a place for formality, it can't all be old-buddy informal stuff and backslapping. But there's also a place for informality. And as chairman, I have to create those two spaces. You don't have to spend too much time creating the formal space because board meetings tend to be structured and formal. So that's fine.
>
> But twice a year, and then I reduced it to once a year, I would have the board come for an evening to have a drink and dinner. We didn't discuss anything in particular. In fact, there were no drinks for the first hour and a half. I had prepared qualitative research as compared to quantitative research, and a set of guidance questions. For example: What do you think of the dynamics of a board? How can we foster more trust? Anybody could answer anything, it had nothing to do with the products or the environment or the margins of the particular company.
>
> By the end of an hour and a half, even the quiet directors had started talking, and the talkative ones had become a bit quieter. Then the drinks tray would come in and we'd have a

drink and we'd continue with this open-ended conversation until someone said, "Hey, let's have dinner." One person was given the task of taking notes because if you record it, people feel hesitant. Then he or she would come and give me the key statements that they noted. And I found that to be invaluable.

Board directors should take steps to build trust. Trust doesn't happen by itself.

///

Ten Questions for the Board of the Future

1. What does the current chair of your board do differently from their predecessors?

2. How solid is the relationship between your company's chair and the chief executive?

3. Can you name three ways in which you think it can be improved?

4. How does the chair of your board (or you, if you are the chair) promote trust and respect among board members?

5. What steps is your chair (or you, if you are the chair) taking to promote diversity of thought on the board?

6. How does your chair (or you, if you are the chair) encourage a frank exchange of views around the boardroom table?

7. Is your chair known for asking questions or for offering advice? (Same question for other board members.)

8. Which of the attributes listed in this chapter do you think will be most valuable for the chair of the future?

9. Name a board chair whom you particularly admire. What does that person bring to the job that makes them stand out?

10. Would you say there is a high degree of trust in your boardroom and with the company's leadership? Is everyone talking to each other truthfully?

CHAPTER TEN

A Plan of Action

In my pre-board work at McKinsey, I spent a lot of time sitting in board meetings related to investments for a North American Pension Fund and an Asian Pension fund, watching a wide mix of board effectiveness—some absolutely terrible boards and some really good boards—and trying to figure out what the key success factors are. You can see whether boards are coherent. Do they have the right skills? Are they clear about what they want to do? How effective is the chair in running the meetings?

—Dominic Barton, chairman, Rio Tinto and LeapFrog Investments

I am by nature an optimist, so I have little doubt that the board of the future will be a vast improvement on its predecessors. Instead of being driven by next quarter's (or even next year's) share price, it will be firmly focused on long-term, sustainable financial performance. This implies that instead of paying attention only to shareholders, it will consider the interests of all who contribute to the business's success. Instead of being dominated by the traditional business establishment, it will draw its members from a more diverse pool carefully defined to help the company execute its strategy. Instead of only counting dollars and cents, it will take seriously its responsibilities to society as a whole, especially the company's impact on scarce natural resources.

Who can disagree that such a transformation will lead to wiser boardroom decisions, wider respect and trust for the business, a more stable workforce and supply chain, and ultimately, yes, an improved bottom line? If enough boards choose to follow this path, we can look forward to a brighter future for the communities where their companies operate and, by extension, for the planet as a whole. As this book tries to spell out, these changes will involve a massive shift in mindsets and in corporate cultures. But I believe that this transition will take place far more quickly than most of us expect.

History is replete with corporate boards that failed to see the future coming, did not move fast enough to adjust to it, and suffered the consequences. Eastman Kodak, Research In Motion (maker of the BlackBerry), British Leyland, Sears Roebuck, and Blockbuster were all once household names that ended up being left in the dust by agile competitors better able to take advantage of the fast-changing world around them. But thankfully, I can count many more cases of far-sighted boards and management teams that have dramatically transformed their businesses, in the process setting an example for all those arriving at similar forks in the road.

Take India's Reliance Group, which made its name as a polyester fabric and petrochemicals producer in the 1970s and '80s but is now the country's largest telecom operator and entertainment group. In Europe, Denmark's largest energy utility, Ørsted, converted itself in little more than a decade from a business centred on coal-fired power plants and offshore oil and gas drilling rigs into a world leader in offshore wind power. Across the Atlantic, IBM (which started life as International Business Machines) has reinvented itself numerous times over the past hundred years. Starting with punch cards and vacuum tubes, it moved on to transistors, mainframe computers, and personal computers and, most recently, has set its sights on artificial intelligence and an open hybrid cloud platform. Even some much-vilified tobacco companies and so-called "oil majors" have seen the writing on the wall and diversified into businesses with more sustainable long-term prospects.

Many more companies will have to go through similar transformations over the next few years. Whether they sink or swim will depend heavily on the quality of their boards. Those that succeed will have a sharply focused mindset. They will keep sustainability, diversity, and the ethical use of technology front and centre, whatever headwinds they may face. They will embrace curiosity and make sure that their members never stop learning. Shailesh Haribhakti, who serves on several boards in the Holcim cement group, singles out one such company:

> Every morning I try to consume one or two webinars or videos or podcasts which put me in touch with examples of the fantastic work that people in the world are doing. One of the great examples is Patagonia, a case study of a competent board. Patagonia made their entire shareholding to be in charge of planet earth. How fantastic an idea is that, that ultimately we are all working towards making sure that life can sustain itself, that biodiversity is respected, that we breathe clean air, and we drink clean water.
>
> If that becomes the way people start thinking, I see a huge breakout in terms of the desire to return to our planet what we have taken away. If we bring all of these tendencies that

are becoming visible and place them in front of the board in a non-confrontational, non-fearful way, then we will get a whole change of mindset, a change of attitude, and it will become a virtuous cycle.

MEASURES OF SUCCESS

It is easy to separate the boards that are making a successful transition to a more sustainable and diverse future from those that are not. Does the company publish an integrated report that draws on both financial and sustainability indicators to determine whether it is creating short- and long-term value? Does it produce evidence of proactive change and innovation, or does it merely recite its compliance with regulations and run-of-the-mill practices? Is diversity of board members, senior executives, and suppliers helping the business execute its strategy, or is it a case of diversity for the sake of diversity? To what extent is the company adhering to the emerging array of international sustainability standards? And so on.

The most far-sighted boards will have a longer time horizon than their predecessors with a vision extending years and perhaps even decades into the future. Andrew Behar of As You Sow sums up the dynamic in many boardrooms and executive suites:

I have conversations with CEOs and they always say, "Oh, I can't do it, because I'll get hurt in the next quarter." I say, "You know, I've got your stock register up on my screen, and I'm scrolling through it. Who exactly are your short-term investors? I'm looking and seeing pension funds, big asset managers, people who hold your stock for ten, twenty, thirty years. I mean, 80 percent of it looks long-term to me. So are you saying that you're making your most strategic decisions based on 10 or 20 percent of your shareholders who are day-trading? If those people sold tomorrow, would you care? Wouldn't it be better for you to be responsive to the folks who are in for the long term?"

Let's stop with this mythology around the next quarter because it really doesn't exist. I think that's starting to sink in.

Some measures of sustainable success may be barely visible to outsiders and apparent only to board members and those close to them. One is the degree of what I call a board's "maturity." As with human beings, maturity is the culmination of a long and arduous process, involving the development of sound relationships between board members and management, a growing measure of insight and foresight, and the many other attributes described in this book. A group of directors who simply nod through every proposal brought before them without asking searching questions is not a mature board. It will reach maturity only when it becomes fully involved in all the stages of drafting a corporate strategy, enabling it to set the future direction of the company. Retired Tata Sons executive director R. Gopalakrishnan highlights the importance of trust and respect:

I would like to see the board move into a different mode, where it is warm, welcoming, and friendly, and encouraging of conversation. That will happen if there is trust, and trust is a product of the heart and the mind. Can they talk freely and not worry about somebody walking out and making a call somewhere? Or passing on information? That's my ideal board of the future.

How should a board engender trust among its members? Several Competent Boards network members emphasize the value of building an esprit de corps. The ways of achieving that will vary from board to board, and from culture to culture. In North America, for example, the Aspen Institute's Erika Karp appreciates being able to give her board colleagues a hug and enjoys having an informal chat with them. But such behaviour may be frowned on in less demonstrative societies. Karp has invited not only legal specialists and climate experts to speak to the boards she serves on, but also a futurist. "You're trying to broaden the vision, broaden the experience of the board," she says. "That's the kind of boardroom I like."

FINALLY ... A CALL TO ACTION

This book outlines the journey of transformation that the board of the future will have to navigate. The combination of established and new competencies highlights a marked shift in boardroom dynamics, aligning the board with the demands of a fast-evolving business environment. By identifying some of the skills that will be required, I hope to lay the groundwork for a more robust, more insightful, and more proactive culture in boardrooms, whatever the size of the company, whatever the sector or country where it operates. An emphasis on digital savviness, an understanding of sustainability, and inclusive, forward-thinking leadership should go a long way towards shaping a boardroom ready to anticipate and respond to the varied challenges and opportunities that lie ahead.

In summary, here are some specific actions that I believe your board could use as a road map for transformation. Following them is an easy-to-read infographic that we at Competent Boards have put together showing ten "must-have" attributes for the future boardroom.

Rethinking board recruitment and composition

Undertake a comprehensive assessment of the competencies represented on the board. The first step is to identify gaps in the context of the emerging business landscape. The assessment should encompass both traditional and future-critical competencies such as digital literacy, a familiarity with sustainability, and current and emerging environmental, social, and governance issues. A forward-thinking mindset is invaluable.

Aim for a diverse board that reflects a variety of perspectives, experiences, and expertise. Consider gender, age, ethnicity, industry experience, and geographical representation in shaping a well-rounded board that can insightfully navigate complex business situations and guide the company towards its strategic priorities.

Use committees sparingly. When specialist expertise is needed, it can often be obtained most effectively from outside advisers rather than from a board committee or new board members.

Set up advisory panels. No matter how competent your board, it will still need help in coming to decisions on some of the complex issues that businesses face these days. Don't hesitate to call in outside experts to help.

Set term limits. No one, no matter how wise or experienced, should be able to measure their length of service on a board in decades.

Give priority to "soft" skills. Demand for future board members will be based less on formal qualifications and job experience than on qualities like curiosity, critical thinking, courage, communication, compassion, and an ability to engage with people from all walks of life.

Set up a regular training program for board members. The goal is to ensure that they remain current on relevant industry trends, regulatory changes, and emerging risks and opportunities. Political and macroeconomic developments should not be forgotten.

Develop a robust succession planning process. It is essential to have a list of qualified candidates for board and key management positions, updated regularly. Succession planning should be aligned with the organization's long-term strategic vision and the board's evolving competency requirements.

Using technology to enhance governance

Embrace safe digital boardroom platforms. These systems can facilitate seamless communication, safe document sharing, and real-time collaboration among board members. By doing so, they can also contribute to more efficient decision-making.

Acquire trusted data analytics and artificial intelligence tools. In this way, the board can use technology to glean actionable insights from data generated by the business, monitor performance, assess risks, and make informed decisions. Use digital twins to test scenarios.

Use the most up-to-date technology to monitor, evaluate, and manage cyber risks. Ensure the board is well informed about the organization's cybersecurity and quantum technology readiness (or lack thereof) and evolving threats.

Engaging beyond the boardroom

Devise a proactive strategy for two-way communication with a broad spectrum of stakeholders. Regular stakeholder engagement can provide valuable insights, build trust, and enhance the organization's reputation. The outreach should be as broad as possible, covering shareholders, employees, customers, suppliers, regulators, and communities in which the company operates or is looking to operate.

Explore informal alliances with industry peers, academic institutions, regulatory bodies, and other stakeholders. Such partnerships can provide fresh insights, foster collaborative problem-solving, and enhance the board's ability to navigate complex industry dynamics. Ensure that you are all on the same page when it comes to advocacy efforts.

Maintain an active, constructive relationship with policymakers and regulators. Keeping in touch with politicians and bureaucrats can facilitate advocacy and simplify compliance with policy decisions. It can also lessen the chance of unpleasant surprises. To that end, inform policy-makers—who, after all, don't know everything—about your company, its priorities, and its achievements.

Pay more attention to local issues. We're moving away from one-size-fits-all to a much more fragmented and localized business world. This could mean taking on a local partner to minimize political risk or, at a more micro level, adapting the company's values to fit in with local cultures.

Cementing a culture of sustainability

Understand where you can make a difference and stay on course. Feedback from stakeholders can often be confusing and even contradictory. Instead of trying to please everyone, which is impossible, the board of the future must stay true to its agreed purpose, focus on the opportunities and threats most material to that purpose, and then communicate them clearly. The stakeholders can then decide if they wish to provide their capital in terms of time, money, and trust to your company.

Keep communicating the benefits of sustainability. Remember, investors and other stakeholders increasingly understand that valuation and reputation are shaped by long-term narratives.

Keep your eye on the long term and adapt. Many boards (and management teams) take the view that if they keep doing what is right today, that strategy will also be right in six months, or in a year or two. That is simply not true. We live in a fast-changing world, and companies need to constantly adapt if they wish to survive.

Use scenario planning. Examining best and worst potential outcomes is one of the most effective ways to prepare for whatever the future may hold, especially costly misadventures.

Set an example to others in your personal behaviour. Board members need to understand that their choices outside the boardroom—what they buy, which causes they support, and, not least, which boards they choose to serve on—all send a message to those around them.

Responding to potential critics of sustainability

Stay cool, calm, and collected. The most successful business leaders and board members are not afraid, angry, or arrogant. They base their strategies on research and knowledge, not on slogans or the fad of the day. An enlightened business does not need to boast about its commitment to "ESG" or "DEI." It just has to do the work to put sensible environmental, social, and governance practices in place. A disciplined strategy and trustworthy information are the best defences against attack.

Show empathy, compassion, and leadership in addressing broad societal issues like economic inequality, mental health, and security. Boards should be open to closer collaboration between companies and governments to address the root causes of these problems and propose initiatives that enhance community engagement and support. In exercising their oversight function, boards should emphasize the importance of embedding core values like empathy and caring within their companies to amplify positive change.

Seek out like-minded allies. This book mentions numerous examples of companies—LEGO, Interface, Patagonia, ExxonMobil, to name a few—that continue to unashamedly drive their businesses to a sustainable future. There are many others, some going about it more quietly than others. The more you can work together with other businesses pursuing the same goals, the more likely that you will succeed not only in accomplishing your purpose but also silencing your critics.

Keep going with the stuff that works. Companies that have thought through their strategy know that they are giving the best value possible to shareholders and other stakeholders. Scenario planning can be a valuable tool in that process. For example, enlightened employment policies enable businesses to attract the brightest talent equipped to give customers what they want today and in the future. So keep going, and don't be shy to report on your strategy, your governance, and your results.

Keep your eye on the big picture and the long game. As directors, your job is to ensure that management is not distracted from the company's overall purpose and goals. An unwavering commitment to enlightened policies, whether labour practices, supplier relationships, or environmental stewardship, will pay off in both financial and non-financial performance measurements, winning respect from a wide swath of stakeholders. As the Heidrick & Struggles report puts it: "Our work reveals that the lessons boards learned by addressing sustainability issues are helping them evolve toward a new model of governance."[104]

10 Must-Haves For Exceptional Board Governance

Cultivate a Culture of Continuous Learning

- Embrace curiosity and humility as catalysts for growth, continually challenging yourselves to expand your horizons and deepen your impact.
- Celebrate your successes, but never rest on your laurels, always striving to raise the bar and set new standards of excellence in governance.

Navigate Risks with Resilience

- Adopt anticipatory thinking and mitigate risks proactively, leveraging the board's collective wisdom and foresight to safeguard the organization's sustainability and reputation.
- Embrace risk as a catalyst for innovation and growth, daring to explore new frontiers while honouring the organization's responsibilities to stakeholders.

Craft a Purpose-Driven Strategy

- Define organization's purpose with clarity, weaving sustainability and societal impact into the organization's core mission.
- Continually refine strategy to adapt to evolving challenges and opportunities, ensuring alignment with the organization's purpose and values.

Curate a Diverse and Empowered Board

- Seek out board members whose diverse perspectives and experiences enrich the discussions and decision-making.
- Empower each board member to contribute their unique expertise, fostering a culture of inclusion and innovation.

Elevate Leadership Excellence

- Appoint a visionary chairperson who not only steers meetings but also inspires collaboration and excellence.
- Cultivate leadership at all levels of the board, nurturing a team of passionate advocates for the organization's mission.

Champion Accountability and Transparency

- Hold yourselves to the highest standards of integrity and accountability, embodying transparency in all actions and communications.
- Embrace constructive feedback and scrutiny as catalysts for growth and improvement, demonstrating the organization's commitment to ethical governance.

Embrace Systems Thinking

- Adopt systems thinking and integrate methodologies like balanced scorecards to connect risks and opportunities across domains, and to enhance understanding of the big picture.
- Utilize systems thinking to navigate and address complexities, ensuring decisions are informed and impactful.

Orchestrate Productive and Purposeful Meetings

- Design meetings that are not just gatherings but transformative experiences, where every voice is heard and every idea is valued.
- Foster robust debates and deliberations, driving toward decisions that are not just good but great for the organization and its stakeholders.

Steer with Strategic Foresight

- Navigate the complexities of the operating environment with strategic foresight, keeping a steady hand on the helm as the board charts the course toward a sustainable future.
- Monitor progress with vigilance, celebrating victories and learning from setbacks as the board strives for continuous improvement

Engage Authentically with Stakeholders

- Forge deep and meaningful connections with stakeholders, listening attentively to their needs and aspirations.
- Co-create solutions that address societal challenges and create shared value, building trust and resilience through authentic engagement.

///

Moving towards a future-ready board calls for reflection, continuing education, and action. The ultimate goal is to ensure that governance structures are strong, adaptable, and in tune with the broader priorities of our society. That is unlikely to happen, however, unless every board member possesses personal qualities that may not be easy to measure nor easy to teach: curiosity, courage, discipline, compassion, and an openness to fresh ideas ... in short, wisdom.

As readers will no doubt have noticed, the foregoing chapters of this book each end with ten questions related to their content. These questions are designed to guide boards on their journey into the future. I hope the answers will help your board identify its current strengths and weaknesses and then fill the gaps. With that in mind, this final chapter ends with just one question:

What are *you* doing to prepare for the future?

Whatever it may be and wherever it may lead, I wish you and your board the very best.

THANK YOU...

As I write these acknowledgments, I think back to the many fantastic leaders, friends, and family members whom I thanked in the prologue to *Stewards of the Future,* my previous book published in 2022. Many of the same people have again generously contributed their thoughts and their time to this project, and I have lots of other names to add.

I'm grateful for all those who are choosing to be part of the solution—the curious and courageous leaders who want to understand how the companies they serve will improve the lives of their stakeholders today and tomorrow, as well as leaving their own businesses in better shape than they found them. I am especially grateful to Diligent, the board governance consultancy, which ordered five thousand copies of *Stewards of the Future* to share with its clients. This new book is a call on every boardroom to be the best it can be by moving from good intentions to excellent performance.

In trying to achieve this goal, I have again had the great pleasure of working with Bernard Simon, who can take my thoughts, ideas, and not-always-so-correct English, and transform them into the words you find in this book. Thank you, Bernard! Also to Ayman Chowdhury for all his help cross-checking the quotes from so many leaders, as well as the data points in this book, and for his great insights and support each and every day.

The Competent Boards network brings together some of the world's smartest and most thoughtful leaders from the worlds of business, social and environmental acumen, and academia. I want to thank those of them who agreed to be interviewed for this book, more than one hundred in all, and the many more who have joined me for Competent Boards network meetings, global dialogue sessions, or just informal chats. Not all of you are mentioned by name in the preceding chapters, but I can assure you that your insights have been invaluable. Special thanks go to:

Agnes K Y Tai, Andrew Behar, Andrew Howard, Anirban Ghosh, Annette Bak Kirby, Byron Loflin, Caroline Casey, Carolynn Chalmers, Chad Holliday, Claudia Sender Ramirez, Daouii Abouchere, David Craig, Dominic Barton, Dottie Schindlinger, Eric Andersen, Eric Wetlaufer, Erika Karp, Faisal Kazi, Francesca Ecsery, Frederic Barge, Jane Diplock, Jingdong Hua, Johan Rockström, Joyce Cacho, Katell Le Goulven, Kathleen Taylor, Khwaja Shaik, Kristjan Jespersen, Maali Khader, Martin Wolf, Meghan Juday, Meredith Sumpter, Mervyn King, Michael Treschow,

Nik Gowing, Pamela Steer, Pat Gallardo Dwyer, Paul Polman, Peter Dey, Philip Upton, Phillip Meyer, R. Gopalakrishnan, Reggie Townsend, Robert Herz, Sarah Kaplan, Sarah Keohane Williamson, Shai Ganu, Shailesh Haribhakti, Tensie Whelan, Torben Möger Pedersen, Yasuhiro Kawasugi, and Yoshiko Shibasaka

Also, a note of appreciation to you, the reader. The transformation of the corporate boardroom is sure to continue at a stunningly rapid pace. With that in mind, I encourage you to share your thoughts and real-life examples of the good, the bad, and the ugly that inevitably mark a period of upheaval and change. **I would much appreciate it if you would use the hashtag #TheFutureBoardroom or share directly with me, so I can share with the Competent Boards network.** Your comments are sure to make the journey more fulfilling for board directors, executives, employees, stakeholders, and the rest of us. Sadly, the world is in a mess, and we need to provide as much support as we can to all those willing and able to be stewards of the future.

Thank you also to all the Competent Boards network members, supporters, and our incredible team. I could not have done this, nor much of my other work, without you.

Finally, a big shout-out goes to my fantastic husband Jesper and daughter Sebrina. Thank you for your patience while I spent countless evenings and weekends working on this book ... and thank you even more for getting me away from my desk to hike, bike, canoe, and enjoy life.

Helle Bank Jorgensen
Toronto, March 2025

ENDNOTES

1. www.stateofglobalair.org/resources/report/state-global-air
   -report-2024

2. www.economist.com/leaders/2024/05/09/the-liberal-
   international-order-is-slowly-coming-apart

3. https://investors.interface.com/news/press-release-details
   /2015/Net-Works-The-worlds-first-inclusive-business-
   model-to-recycle-discarded-fishing-nets-Made-in-the-
   Philippines-and-now-primed-to-go-global/default.aspx

4. https://esgnews.com/orsted-ends-coal-use-closing-last-plant-
   to-achieve-99-green-energy-by-2025/

5. https://orsted.com/en/media/news/2024/01/oersted-
   ranked-the-worlds-most-sustainable-energy--13770950#

6. www.facebook.com/ratantata.aks/posts/business-need
-to-go-beyond-the-interest-of-their-companies-to-the-
communities-th/238179423021912/

7. www.heidrick.com/en/insights/board-of-directors/boards-
and-society-how-boards-are-evolving-to-meet-challenges

8. www.cba.org/Publications-Resources/Practice-Tools/
Business-and-Human-Rights/Business-and-Human-Rights
-as-Law

9. www.cba.org/Publications-Resources/Practice-Tools/
Business-and-Human-Rights/Business-Risk-and-
Corporate-Responsibility/Directors-and-officers-liability
-:~:text=Fiduciary duty of loyalty%3A Directors,would
exercise in comparable circumstances."

10. www.un.org/en/academic-impact/sustainability

11. www.pik-potsdam.de/en/news/latest-news/38-trillion-dollars-
in-damages-each-year-world-economy-already-committed-to-
income-reduction-of-19-due-to-climate-change

12. https://nca2018.globalchange.gov/

13. www.worldwildlife.org/publications/2024-living-planet
-report

14. https://www.qub.ac.uk/News/Allnews/2023/Globallosso
fbiodiversityissignificantlymorealarmingthanpreviously
suspected.html

15. www.lse.ac.uk/granthaminstitute/news/climate-litigation-
against-companies-is-on-the-rise-report-finds/

16. www.mtpr.org/montana-news/2024-01-17/state-regulators
-must-consider-climate-change-during-appeal-of-landmark-
case-supreme-court-says

17. https://dailymontanan.com/2024/12/18/montana-supreme -court-affirms-decision-in-held-historic-youth-climate-case/

18. www.nytimes.com/2024/04/09/world/europe/climate-human-rights.html

19. www.rsm.global/netherlands/en/insights/csrd-uncertainty -national-transpositions-and-eus-drive-regulatory-simplification

20. www.ifrs.org/news-and-events/news/2023/06/issb-issues-ifrs-s1-ifrs-s2/

21. www.ifrs.org/news-and-events/news/2024/11/new-report-global-progress-corporate-climate-related-disclosures/

22. www.efrag.org/en/news-and-calendar/news/efrag-seeks -comments-on-its-draft-endorsement-advice-on-contracts-referencing-naturedependent

23. www.forbes.com/sites/jonmcgowan/2024/10/30/eu-moves -forward-with-drafting-sustainability-reporting-standards-for-non-eu-companies/

24. https://corporatejustice.org/wp-content/uploads/2021/04/ french-corporate-duty-of-vigilance-law-faq-1.pdf

25. https://kpmg.com/us/en/frv/reference-library/2024/ effective-dates-near-for-california-climate-laws.html

26. https://esgnews.com/china-releases-first-corporate-sustainability-disclosure-standards/

27. www.eco-business.com/news/malaysias-issb-consultation-reveals-urgent-need-for-capacity-in-sustainability-reporting/ and www.allenandgledhill.com/sg/publication/ articles/19998/sgx-mandates-climate-and-board-diversity-disclosures

28. www.thomsonreuters.com/en-us/posts/esg/esg-landscape-latin-america

29. www.nortonrosefulbright.com/en/knowledge/publications/730055eb/the-developing-legal-and-regulatory-regime-for-esg-in-the-middle-east-and-emerging-do-exposures

30. www.tamimi.com/news/sca-freshens-up-the-corporate-governance-code-for-uae-listed-companies/ - :~:text=The Amendment Decision provides that,a case by case basis.

31. www.jse.co.za/our-business/sustainability/jses-sustainability-and-climate-disclosure-guidance

32. www.nytimes.com/2024/12/04/business/general-motors-china-electric-vehicles.html?searchResultPosition=1

33. https://clarity.ai/research-and-insights/esg-risk/measuring-esg-risk-esg-controversies-lead-to-a-2-to-5-stock-under performance-after-six-months/#:~:text=Our%20analysis%20covers%20over%2010%2C000,%2D5%25%20after%20six%20months.

34. https://clarity.ai/in-the-news/clarity-ai-esg-controversies-led-to-a-2-to-5-stock-underperformance-after-six-months/

35. www.ft.com/content/8f6f9bc8-2e81-43d0-ad2a-b387de41e0f5

36. www.pwc.com/us/en/services/governance-insights-center/library/annual-corporate-directors-survey.html vey.pdf

37. https://reports.weforum.org/docs/WEF_Global_Risks_Report_2025.pdf

38. www.weforum.org/agenda/2024/05/biodiversity-day-five-priority-actions-for-sectors/ - :~:text=The World Economic Forum's Global,biggest global risk for humanity

39. www.theguardian.com/environment/2023/nov/02/
company-directors-could-be-held-liable-and-fined-over-
unforeseen-nature-related-impacts-and-risks

40. www.theguardian.com/us-news/2024/dec/27/united-
healthcare-brian-thompson-poll

41. www.ft.com/content/f5fe15f8-3703-4df9-b203-
b5d1dd01e3bc

42. www.conference-board.org/press/2024-proxy-season-review-
press-release

43. www.spglobal.com/marketintelligence/en/news-insights/
latest-news-headlines/texas-bans-10-banks-348-investment-
funds-over-fossil-fuel-policies-71842914

44. www.ft.com/content/a76c7feb-7fa5-43d6-8e20-
b4e4967991e7

45. www.blackrock.com/corporate/investor-relations/larry-fink-
annual-chairmans-letter

46. www.wsj.com/business/the-latest-dirty-word-in-corporate-
america-esg-9c776003?mod=hp_lead_pos2

47. https://texasattorneygeneral.gov/news/releases/
attorney-general-ken-paxton-sues-blackrock-state-street-
and-vanguard-illegally-conspiring-manipulate

48. https://uk.finance.yahoo.com/news/lego-scraps-plan-bricks-
recycled-103743725.html

49. www.wsj.com/articles/companies-pledge-action-to-stop
-biodiversity-loss-in-new-initiative-aa3d4489?mod=djem
SustainableBusinessPro&utm_medium=email&_hsenc
=p2ANqtz--8fJK6n3ieTexTHGmHP3KnqPdE7KtGi26a
68gIxvwkuTcy6wiwcEgLhA_fgAAUeiLVJ61F5jDDCCjf-
pDn5RowiwFBa35rGmgvktuqi_JYKtLT9X8&_hsmi=3344
56671&utm_content=334456671&utm_source=hs_email

50. www.economist.com/business/2024/11/14/big-oil-may
-be-softening-its-stance-on-climate-change-regulation?utm
_medium=social-media.content.np&utm_source=twitter
&utm_campaign=editorial-social&utm_content=discovery.
content

51. www.npr.org/2022/07/31/1114796487/

52. https://apnews.com/article/sea-turtles-panama-animal-rights-
world-turtle-day-44cb77ff472ef99cbac7667bce51d38a

53. https://elaw.org/protection-spains-mar-menor

54. www.theguardian.com/environment/2023/aug/26/growing-
number-of-countries-consider-making-ecocide-crime

55. https://www.congress.gov/event/118th-congress/senate-
event/333873/text

56. www.afr.com/companies/financial-services/suncorp-pushes
-big-premium-hike-in-bid-to-grow-profit-margins-20240222
-p5f716 - :~:text=Suncorp pushes big premium increase in
bid to grow profit margins&text=Suncorp has increased car
insurance,profit margins on motor policies

57. www.sec.gov/news/press-release/2023-194

58. www.conference-board.org/publications/addressing-ESG-
backlash

59. www.axios.com/2023/06/26/larry-fink-ashamed-esg-
weaponized-desantis

60. https://corpgov.law.harvard.edu/2023/04/27/does-board-
size-matter/

61. https://www.globenewswire.com/news-release/2024/12/16
/2997653/0/en/US-companies-refine-their-approach-to-ESG
-metrics-in-executive-pay-programs-WTW-study-finds.html

62. www.wtwco.com/en-ca/insights/2024/01/global-report-on-esg-metrics-in-incentive-plans-2023

63. www.iodsa.co.za/page/guidance_for_boards_individual_directors

64. www.iod.com/app/uploads/2024/10/IoD-Code-of-Conduct-for-Directors-October-2024-2e4b026b2f68b2fbf260714c1e08afd3.pdf

65. https://media.frc.org.uk/documents/Cadbury_Code_-_The_Financial_Aspects_of_Corporate_Governance.pdf

66. www.pwc.com/us/en/executive-leadership-hub/board-priorities.html

67. www.idealindustries.com/us/en.html

68. www.leadinggovernance.com/blog/10-things-make-great-board/

69. www.spencerstuart.com/-/media/2024/09/ssbi2024/2024_us_spencer_stuart_board_index_highlights.pdf

70. https://corpgov.law.harvard.edu/2023/12/07/recent-trends-in-board-composition-and-refreshment-in-the-russell-3000-and-sp-500/#:~:text=In percent20the percent20S percent26P percent20500 percent2C percent20it,years percent20in percent20the percent20Russell percent203000

71. www.spencerstuart.com/-/media/2023/september/usbi/2023_us_spencer_stuart_board_index.pdf?sc_trk=BDB9A48933CA433C9DDD7D4E85D62A38

72. https://economictimes.indiatimes.com/news/company/corporate-trends/grey-remains-the-new-black-for-company-boards/articleshow/104029777.cms?from=mdr

73. www.thevaluable500.com/

74. www.nytimes.com/2023/06/29/us/politics/supreme-court-admissions-affirmative-action-harvard-unc.html

75. https://fortune.com/2023/07/15/affirmative-action-13-republican-attorney-general-letter-corporate-ceos-fortune-100/

76. www.livenowfox.com/news/companies-roll-back-dei-policies

77. www.wsj.com/articles/chief-diversity-officer-cdo-business-corporations-e110a82f?page=1

78. www.blackrock.com/corporate/literature/fact-sheet/blk-responsible-investment-guidelines-us.pdf

79. www.agendaweek.com/c/4725214/632614/blackrock_axes _board_diversity_requirements_guidelines?referrer_module =emailMorningNews&module_order=0&code=YUdKcVF HTnZiWEJsZEdWdWRHSnZZZWEprY3k1amIyMH NJREV5TlRFNU9EZzBMQ0F4TVRFM056QTBNakk1

80. https://asia.nikkei.com/Business/Artificial-intelligence-gets-a-seat-in-the-boardroom

81. www.goldmansachs.com/intelligence/pages/generative-ai-could-raise-global-gdp-by-7-percent.html

82. www.ibm.com/thought-leadership/institute-business-value/en-us/report/business-trends-2025

83. www.forbes.com/sites/forbestechcouncil/2023/05/30/reinventing-anti-money-laundering-how-federated-learning-can-power-fund-diversion-detection-and-gdpr-compliance/?sh=3ff50ae63341

84. https://doi.org/10.1016/j.cose.2022.102840

85. www.diligentinstitute.com/report/cybersecurity-audit/

86. www.ibm.com/reports/data-breach?utm_content=SRCW
W&p1=Search&p4=43700067972513691&p5=p&p9=
58700007546740765&gad_source=1&gclid=Cj0KCQiAv
P-6BhDyARIsAJ3uv7ZB4R2a1_rYomzhj5qpaFuFDrtzYm
P6gVodJW5ezyZ5mFK55NdvaMwaAjh4EALw_wcB&gc
lsrc=aw.ds

87. https://securityintelligence.com/articles/roundup-the-top-
ransomware-stories-of-2024/

88. www.sec.gov/files/rules/final/2023/33-11216.pdf

89. www.cpacanada.ca/business-and-accounting-resources/
other-general-business-topics/information-management
-and-technology/publications/questions-directors-should-
ask-about-cybersecurity

90. https://apnews.com/general-news-ecfb398fa555456d99fe
40e0a05dd1da

91. www.pwc.com/gx/en/services/forensics/disruption
-podcast-series/14-deepfakes-disinformation-disrupting-
corporate-sector.html

92. https://corpgov.law.harvard.edu/2023/10/07/ai-and-the-
role-of-the-board-of-directors/

93. www.directorsandboards.com/board-issues/ai/the-ups-and-
downs-of-generative-ai-for-boards

94. https://www.pensiondanmark.com/en/investments/active-
ownership-and-responsible-investments/

95. www.mandg.com/investments/professional-investor/en-gb
/insights/mandg-insights/latest-insights/2024/03/engagement
-and-investor-additionality-in-impact-investing; https://
www.nlc.health/insight/the-power-of-additionality-why-
impact-investing-should-focus-on-building-companies-that-
otherwise-wouldnt-exist

96. www.fca.org.uk/publications/policy-statements/ps23-16-
sustainability-disclosure-requirements-investment-labels

97. www.clientearth.org/latest/press-office/press/clientearth
-files-climate-risk-lawsuit-against-shell-s-board-with-
support-from-institutional-investors/

98. www.theguardian.com/business/2023/jul/24/clientearth-
high-court-fight-shell-climate-strategy-net-zero

99. www.theguardian.com/business/2023/jul/24/clientearth-
high-court-fight-shell-climate-strategy-net-zero

100. www.ifc.org/content/dam/ifc/doc/mgrt/publicconsultation.
pdf

101. www.cnbc.com/2024/06/21/shein-us-ipo-is-dead-experts-
say.html

102. https://hbr.org/2021/11/6-types-of-resilience-companies-
need-today#:~:text=Net%2Dpositive%20companies%20
build%20better,simply%20demanding%20the%20
lowest%20cost

103. https://blogs.insead.edu/idpn-globalclub/modern-chair-
practices-what-makes-an-effective-board-chair/

104. www.heidrick.com/en/insights/board-of-directors/boards-
and-society-how-boards-are-evolving-to-meet-challenges

INDEX

A

Abouchere, Daouii 88, 90, 109, 118, 141
accountability 88, 211
activists 167–170
adaptability 68, 177, 208
"additionality" 169
advisory panels 205
agendas 74, 191–192
age of directors 125–127
agility 79–80
Andersen, Eric 63
Anderson, Ray xvi
artificial intelligence (AI)
    benefits versus risks 155–160
    checklist 160–161
    demand for 139
    ethics and 77, 144–146
    generative 143
    governance and 191, 206–207
    predictive 143
    privacy and 145
    rewards 139
    risks 142–144
    robo-director 137–138
    sustainability and 142
    uses of 140, 141–142
Australia 63–64

B

backsliding 21–24
Bak Kirby, Annette 73, 122
Bank Jorgensen, Helle xvi, 1
Barge, Frederic 82, 83
Barton, Dominic 76, 78, 199
Behar, Andrew 52, 58, 80, 175, 180, 202
bias 145

biodiversity, loss of 7–8
BlackRock 56, 57, 69, 133
board chair
    agenda and 191–192
    attributes of 192–195
    CEO relationship and 188–189
    role of 189–191
    trust and truth and 195–197
board composition
    changing nature of 95–96
    community reflection 124
    diversity, equity, and inclusion
        (DEI) xiii, 121–123, 127–129,
        131–135, 211
    expertise 129–131
    rethinking 205–206
board/management interaction
    115–116, 118–119
bodies of water 62
Brazil 18
briefing materials 87
Brundtland Commission 4
Bud Light 9

C

Cacho, Joyce 40–41, 79, 100,
    134, 146
California 17, 63, 109–111
call to action 204–212
Casey, Caroline 128
CEO 188–189, 190
chair of the board 185–188
Chalmers, Carolynn 39, 106
China 17
circular business model 66
Citizens Property Insurance
    Corporation 63
ClientEarth 169–170
climate change
    business role in solutions 7

constitutional rights 13
disclosure law 17
economic impact 6–7
insurance and 63
lawsuits 12–13
nature loss and 8
Coca-Cola 151
Code of Conduct for Directors 87
Colombia 18
committees
    number of 79–80, 205
    role of 78–79
    types of 76–78
communication 67, 68, 115, 116,
    161, 162, 171, 179, 207
Competent Boards xi–xii
complexity 67
compliance
    AI and 140
    committee 77
    whistle-blowing and 117
compromise 178
Conference Board 68, 69
conformity 156
corporate social responsibility
    xxi–xxii, 3, 10–11
    See also environmental, social,
    and governance (ESG)
corporation size xix–xx
*Cost of a Data Breach Report
    2024* 147
courage 117–118
CPA Canada 150
Craig, David 8, 48
credentials 108
critical outcomes 30–31
culture wars 56, 132–133
curiosity 40
cyber-resilience 149–150
cybersecurity 207
    board roles 148

costs of 147
value creation and 148–149

D

Danish Oil and Natural Gas
 (DONG) xvi–xvii
Dark Angels 147
deadwood 110
decision making 124–125
deepfakes 151, 153, 154, 161–162
Deep Knowledge Ventures 138
Deutsche Bank 64–65
Dey, Peter 190, 193
digital revolution *See* technology
Diplock, Jane 23, 37, 41, 105,
 106, 107, 126
director, corporate
 age of 125–127
 CEO relationship and 190
 duties of 194
 expanding role of 2–3
 personal behaviour 209
 personal purpose 73
 responsibility for change
  xxi–xxii, 2, 10–11
 skills/characteristics 30, 34,
  35–36, 37–38, 89–90, 96,
  114, 205
 soft skills 38–42
 stewardship role of x–xi, 3–4,
  118
 working role of xii–xiii
disabilities 128
disclosure standards 15
disinformation 151, 152, 154
diversification 200–201
diversity, equity, and inclusion
 (DEI)
 backlash 154
 benefits of 134–135

board chair and 191
board composition xiii,
 121–123, 127–129, 131–135,
 205, 211
culture wars 132–133
defined x
need for more 131
new definitions of 127–129
technology and 140–141
tokenism 132
transformation and 123
understanding 122
DSM 82

E

ecocide 62
Ecsery, Francesca 84, 124, 156,
 192
efficiency 74–75
Eileen Fisher 93
electric cars 51–52
environmental, social, and
 governance (ESG)
 in Africa 19
 backlash 154
 blowback 55–57
 in China 17
 defined x
 as good business 11
 greenwashing 64–65
 in Latin America 18
 laws relating to 62
 lawsuits 23, 57
 measurements of 18
 pervasiveness of 49–52
 reporting metrics 28–29
 terminology 68–69
Ericsson 82
ethics 77–78, 144–146
European Financial Reporting

Advisory Group (EFRAG) 16
expertise 129–131
ExxonMobil 60

F

fairness 88
FAIR Plan 63
family business 109–111
federated machine learning 140
feedback 111
financial acumen 96
Fink, Larry 57, 69
Firmenich 82
flexibility 21
Florida 63
forward thinking 41–42
future
changes on the horizon 85–88
preparing for 34–38
turbulent times ix–xxii

G

Gallardo Dwyer, Pat 31
Ganu, Shai 81
Ghosh, Anirban 39, 42, 45, 93
Goldman Sachs 139, 193
Gopalakrishnan, R. 35, 39, 42,
96, 102, 108, 118, 144, 174,
175, 185, 196, 203
governance
critical outcomes 30–31
good behaviour and 39
improvement, demand for
14–15
must-haves 211
outcomes-based governance
28–31
purpose 31–34
shifting landscape 55–71
stakeholders in 12

sustainable 57–60
technology and 206–207
Gowing, Nik 155
greenhushing 152–154, 162
greenwashing 64–65
green wishing 88
Gregory, Holly 152
Guidance for Boards 86

H

Haribhakti, Shailesh 35, 102, 187,
201
*Harvard Law School Forum on
Corporate Governance* 152
Harvard University 132
healthcare 50, 51
Herz, Robert 121, 134
Hindu philosophy 35
Holliday, Chad 27, 28, 44, 50, 51,
52, 79, 104, 105, 125
honesty 36, 87, 101–102,
195–197
Howard, Andrew 116, 119, 129
Hua, Jingdong 20

I

IBM 139, 147, 200–201
Ideal Industries 109–111
IFRS S1 15
IFRS S2 15, 20
incentives
broad-based approach to 84–85
factors to consider 83–85
short-/long-term 82–83
for sustainability performance
80–82
inclusive capitalism 11
inclusiveness 39
insurance 62–64
integrity 87

Interface xvi
International Financial Reporting
  Standards (IFRS) 15, 18, 20
International Sustainability
  Standards Board 15, 20

J

Jakobsdóttir, Katrín 62
Jarislowsky, Stephen 101
Jenkins, Michael 112
Jespersen, Kristjan 46, 50, 96
John Deere 105
Juday, Meghan 110

K

Kaplan, Sarah 189, 191
Karp, Erika 30, 33–34, 179, 204
Kawasugi, Yasuhiro 179
Kazi, Faisal 107, 150, 157
Keohane Williamson, Sarah 55
Khader, Maali 12, 41, 128
Kinder Morgan 175–177
King, Mervyn 30, 31, 40, 101,157,
  165, 178, 181–182, 187, 193

L

Latin America 18
leadership 87, 186–188, 211
Leading Governance 114
learning, continuous 105–108,
  111, 211
leasing xix, 66
LEGO Group 59
Lehman Brothers 178
LGBTQ+ community 9
listening 165–166
Loflin, Byron 107, 129–130,
  160
long-term view 202–203, 208,
  210

Loon, Karen 192
Lorsch, Jay 129–130

M

Maersk xvii–xviii
management/board interaction
  115–116, 118–119
Mar Menor 62
maturity 203
measures of success 202–204
meetings 115, 211
mentoring, reverse 107
Meyer, Phillip 3
micromanager 113
misinformation 151
Mission Possible Partnership
  43–44
modern slavery laws 3
Möger Pedersen, Torben 9, 10,
  169
Mother Nature xxvi, 61 *See also*
  nature-related issues
Mulvaney, Dylan 9

N

natural resources, exploitation of 8
nature-related issues
  business opportunities 47
  catastrophic events 61
  climate. See climate change
  financial disclosures 8, 47
  GDP and 44–45
  global risk 45
  insurance and 62–64
  place at the table 44–49
  priority on xvii, 48–49 *See also*
    climate change
Nigeria 5–6
Novo Nordisk 172–173

O

obstacles 131–135
Ørsted xvi–xvii, 200
outcomes-based governance 28–31

P

Panama 61–62
Patagonia 201–202
Pedersen, Torben Möger 159
PensionDanmark 169
performance
  balanced with purpose 67
  evaluation of 110
  incentives and 80
  measurement of 81–82, 87–88
personality types 112–113
planning 74
politics 8–10
Polman, Paul 22, 111, 123, 181
priorities 2–4, 68
privacy, AI and 145
purpose
  of board 31–34
  personal 73

Q

questioning xii, 30, 110, 115, 160, 174, 179–180

R

"radar and response" model 174
Rebien Sørensen, Lars 172
recruitment 38–39, 205
regulation
  advocacy for 161–162
  in the future 60–61
  increase in 14–21
  Sustainability Disclosure Requirements 169

Trump intent to loosen 16–17
rejuvenation 42–43
Reliance Group 200
responsibility for change xxi–xxii, 2
responsible business 88
reverse mentoring 107
rights
  of bodies of water 62
  climate change and 13
risks
  navigating 211
  risk and compliance committee 77
robo-director 138
Rockström, Johan 6
Roddick, Anita 175
Royal Dutch Shell 51, 169–170

S

Saudi Arabia 18–19
scenario planning 209
Schindlinger, Dottie 149
Science Based Targets Network 59–60
sea turtles 61–62
Sender Ramirez, Claudia 117, 126, 137, 143, 165, 167
Shaik, Khwaja 146, 148
shareholders 165, 167, 176
Shein 173–174
Shibasaka, Yoshiko 91
size of board 75–76
skills/characteristics
  continuous learning 105–108
  curiosity and willingness to learn 34
  diversity of experience 103
  financial acumen 96
  in greatest demand 101–105
  identifying 205
  importance of 89–90

initiative 97–98
list of 35, 37–38, 99, 114
moral/intellectual/spiritual
  capital 35–36
questioning 30
skills matrix 37–38, 89–90, 124
soft skills 38–42, 101, 102, 206
specialists 128–129
stakeholder engagement
benefits of 168, 181–182,
  207–208
committee 78
good practices 170–180
importance of 166, 211
stakeholder inclusive approach
86–87, 161
statement of purpose 33
Steer, Pamela 150
stewardship x–xi, 3–4, 118
Stewards of the Future (Bank
  Jorgensen) xiv–xv, 1, 171
strategy 65–70, 158–159, 211
succession planning 89, 125, 206
Sumpter, Meredith 11, 50–51
Suncorp 63–64
sustainability
backsliding, cost of 21–24
benefits of 92–93
board expertise 42–43
as core business driver 67
critics, responding to 209–210
culture of 208–209
International Sustainability
  Standards Board 15, 20
in Middle East 18–19
no going back 60–62
performance and 80–85, 88
permanence of 57–60
priority of 90–93
reporting 16, 50
sense of purpose and 33–34

standards 15, 17
strategies for the future 65–70
success and 4
technology and 142
terminology 68–69
value creation and 11
Switzerland 13
systems thinking 211

T

Tai, Agnes 15
Taskforce on Nature-related
  Financial Disclosures (TNFD)
  8, 47, 48
Tata, Jamsetji 181
Tata, Ratan xxi
Taylor, Kathleen 2, 41, 74, 75, 87,
  89–90, 95, 101, 107, 142
technology
artificial intelligence. *See*
  artificial intelligence (AI)
  board roles 148, 155–156,
  159–160, 161–163
cybersecurity 146–150
diversity and 140–141
ethics and 144–146
governance and 206–207
rewards 139–142
risks 142–144
robo-director 138
strategies for the future 158
  159
sustainability and 142
underbelly of 150–152
Tensie Whelan 131, 132
terminology 68–69
term limits 125–127, 206
Texas 69
titles 100
tokenism 132

Townsend, Reggie 160
Toxic Humans (Jenkins) 112
toxic leadership 112–114
training 108, 159–160, 161, 206
transformation 123, 200–202,
04, 205–212
transition investing 57
transition plan 108–109, 119
transparency 35, 88, 161, 211
Treschow, Michael 21, 64, 78,
114, 125, 128, 189, 195
Trump, Donald ix, 60
trust 195–197, 203–204
turbulent times ix–xxii

U

United Arab Emirates 18
UnitedHealthcare, CEO murder
51
University of North Carolina 132
Upton, Philip 151

V

Valuable 500 128
value creation 11
Vedanta philosophical tradition 35
"vigilance plan" 16
VITAL 138
von der Leyen, Ursula 14

W

Wetlaufer, Eric 28, 45, 81, 102,
115, 160, 177
Whelan, Tensie 28, 29, 82, 91,
104, 190
whistle-blowers 117
Winston, Andrew 181
wokeness 55–56, 132

Wolf, Martin 1, 10
Woods, Darren 60
World Economic Forum 44, 47

Y

You Sow 175

ABOUT THE AUTHOR

Helle Bank Jorgensen, the CEO and founder of Competent Boards, is an internationally recognized voice on sustainable governance practices.

A business lawyer and certified public accountant by training, Helle is a member of the Nasdaq Center for Board Excellence; the World Economic Forum Expert Network for Corporate Governance, Leadership, and Emerging Multinationals; and the co-chair of the global expert panel Accounting for Sustainability established by King Charles III.

A native of Denmark, Helle has lived in the United States and Canada, where she was named one of Canada's Most Powerful Women in 2022 and recognized by *The Globe and Mail* as a "Global Changemaker" in 2023. In 2024, she received the Corporate Governance Lifetime Achievement Award in New York City. In November 2024, *IR (Investor Relation) Magazine* inducted her into the Corporate Governance Hall of Fame.

Board members and executives in over 55 countries—many from Fortune 500 companies—have achieved certification from Competent Boards. They have gone on to help their companies mitigate the risks and seize the opportunities presented by the ever-evolving governance landscape.

Helle's Amazon bestseller *Stewards of the Future: A Guide for Competent Boards* was published in 2022 and has sold nearly 10,000 copies. She is a regular contributor to the *Financial Times'* FT Agenda and Board Agenda, and has been interviewed by many leading publications. Prior to founding Competent Boards, she was a partner at PwC.